The Turning Word

Critical Authors & Issues

Josué Harari, Series Editor

The Turning Word

American Literary Modernism and
Continental Theory

Joseph N. Riddel

Edited with an Introduction by Mark Bauerlein

PENN

University of Pennsylvania Press

Philadelphia

Copyright © 1996 by the University of Pennsylvania Press
All rights reserved
Printed in the United States of America

Library of Congress Cataloging-in-Publication Data

Riddel, Joseph N.
    The turning word : American literary modernism and continental theory /
Joseph N. Riddel : edited by Mark Bauerlein.
        p.   cm.
    Includes bibliographical references and index.
    ISBN 0-8122-3378-6 (alk. paper).—ISBN 0-8122-1600-8 (pbk. alk. paper)
    1. American poetry—20th century—History and criticism—Theory, etc. 2.
Philosophy in literature. 3. Modernism (Literature)—United States. 4. H.D.
(Hilda Doolittle), 1886–1961—Philosophy 5. Crane, Hart, 1899–1932—
Philosophy. 6. Stein, Gertrude, 1874–1946—Philosophy. 7. Olson, Charles,
1910–1970—Philosophy. 8. American poetry—European influences. 9.
Poetry. I. Bauerlein, Mark. II. Title.
PS310.P46R54 1996
811'.5209—dc20   96-23328
                                                                  CIP

PS310
.P46
R54
1996

Contents

Introduction

Mark Bauerlein

The essays collected here embody Joseph N. Riddel's culminating meditations upon literary theory and modern American literature. They develop a theme explored in a summary essay Riddel composed just after publishing his theoretical study of William Carlos Williams's poetics (*The Inverted Bell*), that essay here reproduced as chapter 1, "Doubling and Poetic Language: Heidegger and Derrida." That theme is the relation of philosophy to literature, of conceptual thought to poetic form. From the late 1970s onward, Riddel understood much of his work (amounting during this time to over twenty-five essays and reviews) as a meditation on this theme, a series of speculations headed toward a decisive interpretation of modernist writing. Just before his untimely death in 1991, Riddel organized one line of interrogation into a book, with the essays positioned as follows under the title *The Turning Word*.

Riddel's titular epithet signifies language's tropic capacity, its deflection from figure to figure, a metaphorical slippage that unsettles conceptual stability. While philosophical discourse strives for a precise and unambiguous expression of concepts, it must use words that are prone to turn away from the ideas they are supposed to represent. When a word will not remain in a one-to-one correspondence with a referent, when for reasons of context or convention or rhetoric a word will not stay still, then it disobeys philosophy's mandate that words denote faithfully. The philosophical upshot of language's semantic infirmity is, to use the Heideggerean language Riddel often resorts to, that the "turning word" enacts a "performative displacement of classical concepts of Being." What is a "performative displacement"? A language becomes performative and displaces Being when it turns from a linear referentiality, when its words effect a rhetorical action, when they do something other than simply refer denotatively. This is when words become playful, ambivalent, poetic, figurative—often, as in the case of much modernist writing, poetic and figurative to the extent that the poetry-prose, figurative-literal distinction breaks down.

Philosophy presents an array of systematic strategies for appraising the representational trustworthiness of words, judging their truth-value, transparency, logicality, and grammar in terms of correspondence and/or coherence. But philosophy from Plato to early Wittgenstein offers few strategies of evaluating the performative effects of words, of classifying its turns, except by excluding it as non-philosophical. John Austin's powerful exploration of performance may be seen as a distinctive attempt to circumscribe performance and induct it into philosophy. However, he does so not by analyzing the "turning" action of words, but rather by recounting the context of their utterance. That is, Austin delimits performativity by focusing on the situations in which words perform. In so doing, Austin invokes a philosophical language that regulates performative language's operations, that offers a set of standards substituting "happiness" and "unhappiness" for truth and falsity, thereby ensuring a descriptive and stable assessment of performances.

While respecting Austin's achievement, Riddel finds, such philosophical descriptions of performatives inadequate in relation to the performances of modernist writing. His close readings of Pound, Crane, Stein, and so on show how modernism's performative acts unleash language from the situational and sincerity constraints Austin would bring to bear on them. He isolates the modern as neither a concept nor a meaning, but rather a performative act not fully explicable by a conceptual or semantic analysis. He then proceeds to focus on the modernist word's most explicit occasion of turning: when philosophy meets poetry. Hence, the chapters following the Heidegger-Derrida essay contain analyses of four philosopher-poet relationships: Freud and H.D., Hegel and Hart Crane, Bergson and

Gertrude Stein, and poststructuralism and modernist-postmodern poetry, mainly Charles Olson. Against the philosophers' dialectical or analytical directions, the poets, Riddel finds, cause an uncanny disorientation of philosophy's pursuit of transparency and truth. Hailing the intervention of words and images and long poems that cannot be entirely reduced to conceptual descriptions, Riddel's modern poets repeatedly implicate philosophy's extraction of concepts from performances in performative processes. That is, modernist poets position concepts in strategies of translation, interpretation, and writing.

But this does not mean that modernist poetry has achieved a pre-conceptual immediacy of experience or a non-conceptual expression of motive or feeling. Even Hegel, grandfather of poststructuralist thinking, said that art was "the sensuous presentation of the Idea." Poetry does not annul philosophy. Instead, it activates philosophical ideas, situates the idea in the act. H.D., Hart Crane, Stein, and Olson recast philosophical discourse not as the definition of abstract concepts, but as acts of vision and interpretation. Modernism does not close the book of philosophy and yield a world of pure acts of the mind or will. Rather, modernism acts as a new critical discourse, one that tries not to overcome the old work, but to perform it differently, more consciously and playfully. Critically involved in what it revises, modernism has no ex-position from which to mount an exposition—it only plays the game of concepts inventively, poetically, taking turns.

This readjustment of the interpretive aims of modern criticism and modern literature is perhaps the strongest programmatic thrust of Riddel's book. The readings he does of modern American poetry are detailed, complex, and exacting—and they are original and adept. Though published some years ago, these chapters deserve publication as a coherent and formative study of American modernism. The Heidegger-Derrida piece appeared in *boundary 2* twenty years ago, but it still holds up well despite the putative progress literary criticism has made beyond the theoretical concerns of the 1970s. Not only does it economically set up the philosophy-poetry problematic carried out by the rest of these explications, but few essays in the history

of literary theory speak as judiciously and competently about
the philosophical underpinnings of deconstruction as Riddel's
does. The chapters on H.D., Crane, Stein, and Pound and
Olson are similarly thoughtful and innovative. Few other published works have taken these poets as seriously—as seriously
playful thinkers—as these readings do. In the chapter on
Crane, Riddel's introduction of Hegel and everything Hegel
connotes (totalization, transcendence, the end of art) into
American poetics subtly throws into relief the syntheses, the
crossings, the bridgings necessary to Hegelian thought, indeed,
to any systematic philosophy or historicism. The analysis of
Stein is a sustained and careful philosophical commentary on
her poetry and poetics, on Bergsonian subjective time and
Steinian "ego-graphy," perhaps the best analysis of her work in
these terms yet written. And Riddel's opening discussion in the
last chapter of the relation of modernism to postmodernism
(partly posed as a relation between Pound and Olson) is a clear
and useful theorization of the latter phenomenon, despite postmodernism's notorious indeterminacy. What these readings do
is understand and judge the poets as thinkers, to be sure, as
anti-philosophical thinkers, but nevertheless, as writers thinking philosophical questions and concepts—totality, truth, consciousness, the unconscious, representation—through to anti-
philosophical conclusions. This marks a new possibility for ap-
preciating American modernism.

   Some readers may be impatient with Riddel's mode of critical analysis. New historicist, new Americanist, and cultural critics may wonder why criticism should concern itself with such
rarefied issues as the interaction of image and concept, the action of metaphor in philosophical language, the nature of poetic performance. Language is a representation, one historically and socially determined, they avow. So, criticism should
examine those determinations to see how they select certain
objects and persons for representation, and to see what values
get attached to those representations. That is, in literary criticism, the politics of representation should prevail over the theory of representation. What should be the focus of analysis are
race, class, and gender representations, not the semantics and
semiotics of representation per se.

Riddel would not wholly disagree with this line of reasoning. What ultimately counts are the social, political, and personal effects of art and criticism should try to make those various consequences as explicit and clear as possible. However, Riddel would say, that imperative is not so easy to follow when it comes to American modernism. The representations in Pound's *Cantos*, in Stein's "Composition as Explanation," in Crane's *The Bridge*, and so on are too complicated, ironic, and ambivalent to allow for a simple extraction of representational content from them. Before critics can determine, say, the politics of H.D.'s analysis of Freud's analysis of her, they must take into account H.D.'s interrogation of the methods and purposes of analysis per se, particularly, in Freud's case, the reliance of analysis on mythological and literary narratives. If Freud himself proclaimed that the poets discovered the unconscious long before he did, if H.D. herself turns the analysis of the neurotic poet back upon the analyst himself, then what status can an analytical reading of her *Tribute to Freud* have? Until that critical question is worked out, H.D.'s text remains at least partially ignored. Indeed, Riddel would argue, its very modernism is overlooked, for such interpretive problems, especially those centered on the poetry-philosophy, creative-critical opposition, are modernism's distinguishing feature. So, because criticism in general operates on precisely that distinction, criticism of modernist writing must proceed hyper-self-consciously, ever mindful of its own critical gestures, since much of the material under study anticipates those gestures and treats them ironically, skeptically, poetically. Like H.D.'s remembrance, modernist texts work against the analytical grain (to the conventional critic's unending frustration). They demand that scholars maintain a thoroughgoing theoretical sedulousness, one that will attend to the performative media and unstable contexts of modernist representations, as well as to their socio-political content.

Riddel's interpretations address exclusively the former obligation. In doing so, however, they do not contradict political or new historical criticism of modernism. Instead, Riddel's readings complement them. Specifically, Riddel explores theoretical complications the latter methodologies bypass (sometimes for good political reasons, other times out of basic disinterest).

Uncertain as to exactly what relation obtains in modernist representations between form and content, tradition and originality, America and Europe, and so on, he holds off on drawing thematic conclusions about modernist writing until he has detailed those themes' interpretive framing, the language that expresses them, the experimental styles and forms that unfold yet also displace the themes' central concepts. And Riddel does so not to forestall those conclusions, but only to give them a sounder theoretical basis. Modernism solicits that theoretical hesitation, that anxiety about interpretation; and if Riddel's work is to be recognized as worthwhile in a critical climate that commends the easy translation of formal complexity into political content, then it will be because the literature will not let that translation proceed smoothly. To skirt modernism's disturbance of conventional reading habits, particularly reading's reliance on philosophical concepts, would be to repress one of modernism's most significant qualities. Riddel's work must be read as an alternative to that outcome.

Chapter One
Doubling and Poetic Language: Heidegger and Derrida

I

American criticism has come to Heidegger, or he to it, very late, and for the most part by indirection. The detour produces a certain, inevitable distortion, like the itinerary of a translation, though it may be no more than the inevitable misinterpretation already posited in the Heideggerean hermeneutic. On the other hand, this lateness circumvents not a few historical distractions. While our philosophers have had to confront the politics as well as the language of Heidegger, literary criticism has been able to ignore the kind of resistances which mark in one way or another almost every reading of Heidegger in Europe—the political resistances which conceal deeper resistances, and reciprocally. Derrida remarks in various places upon the apparent obligation to begin a consideration of Heidegger with a kind of apologetics for the political and/or ideological contaminations that threaten his readers. We have been spared this for the most part, only perhaps because we have been spared a direct Heideggereanism.

But we have not been spared the problems of a certain historical seamlessness. What historians of modern thought have come to distinguish as two Heideggers (the destroyer of metaphysics and the celebrant of poetic "dwelling"), we have received in a more or less single package of transcriptions which tend to suppress the difference, or at least to remove it as a primary concern for literary criticism. Beyond that question, however, another one arises. Presuming two Heideggers, even if one is continuous with the other, do the two lend themselves to a unified hermeneutical method? It is not my concern here to take up the question of this historical placing of an early and late Heidegger, and certainly not to consider the sameness and difference in any evolution of his thought.

The task here is much more modest—to remark the place of Heidegger in certain projects of literary criticism. But for this purpose, one cannot ignore that the commercial (Heidegger might say, "technological") chance of his translation into English texts has provided his thought with a kind of interpretive framing—the appearance in the early fifties of parts of the Holderlin book, combined with the later translations of Heidegger on language and poesis, bookending the earliest and basic text, *Being and Time.* Setting this historical dislocation aside leaves the other fact that whatever impact Heidegger has had on literary criticism comes not so much directly from his own critical writings, via comparatist critics alert to the intellectual dialogue in Europe, as by another indirection: the absorption of the Heideggerean hermeneutic into various European criticisms, from existentialism to the "criticism of consciousness" to structuralism. In particular, one would have to say that the so-called Geneva school, which has had an indelible impact on American criticism, again by a certain indirection, is situated in a critique of "consciousness" and "place" which is at the same time undergirded and undermined by Heidegger's early writing. But at the very moment that a "criticism of consciousness," with its phenomenological orientation, had begun to offer a fruitful alternative to American formalist and thematic criticism, another kind of formalism known as structuralism, directed explicitly at the ground of phenomenology, the priority of consciousness, had begun to be translated into a variety of American methodologies.

What has been missing from the American debate, however, except in the work of a few critics with deep continental roots, is the considerable history of hermeneutical thinking which has crisscrossed Europe in the last hundred years. At the center of that thinking has been the Heideggerean destruction of metaphysics, but no less the retrieval and reinterpretation of

Hegelian and Nietzschean thought, the appropriation of psychoanalysis by philosophy, and the centering of criticism on the problematics of language opened up by the new linguistics. The history is familiar enough in its broader outlines, though for the most part the American critic's awareness of the dialogue between phenomenology and structuralism has been so foreshortened that the intellectual consequences of the confrontation have been repressed. The dialogue has come so late to the American academy that, with certain powerful exceptions, we find ourselves in a poststructuralist period without having suffered the rites of initiation into that which it has displaced. This can lead to superficial jokes about the abbreviated half-life of the Parisian element of ideas. It is disconcerting, after all, to be reminded that within a singular deployment of a hermeneutical method derived in part from Heidegger (and from Nietzsche and Freud), translated as a destruction, or more precisely, as a deconstruction of metaphysics, we may find so much lumped into one grand metaphysical heap: Platonic idealism and Aristotelian formalism; all the varieties of subjectivism from Descartes through Hegel and Nietzsche, which we recognize in one form or other of romanticism or dialectical thought; phenomenology (which thought to escape the subject-object problem), existentialism, and structuralism; and finally, even the deconstructors themselves (especially Heidegger). In short, all western (Heidegger called it "onto-theological") thought, including that of those who have tried to overthrow metaphysics, is combined into a deconstruction and then celebrated, condemned, reenacted, misrepresented, used and/or abused.

Every move of this nonhistory of ideas surpasses and displaces a previous move. In a succession of moves that now reveal something more like a game of chess than a progress of knowledge, we experience a foreshortened history of ideas that culminates in a variety of attempts to close metaphysics and overthrow it, appropriate it, or, more radically, step outside it: Nietzsche's naming of Hegel as the end of metaphysics; Husserl's dream to write its closure; Heidegger's reading of Nietzsche's will to power as the ultimate subjectivism; and the revival of the Nietzschean question of interpretation in the work of Foucault, Deleuze, and Derrida. Derrida, in fact, in an essay entitled "Les Fins de l'homme," calls this latest overthrow by the name of "France" or "French thought" (in contrast, obviously, to the closures of German thought, particularly Heidegger's).[1] Have we, in and through these names, arrived at the "end of philosophy" which Heidegger long since announced as Nietzsche's *capital* achievement? And arrived there by the disruption achieved in the Derridean deconstruction of Heidegger's destruction?

The question, which could be made portentous, is obviously beyond our asking here. But a more modest question can be posed. Translated over into a more limited field, what does this deconstruction of metaphysics, or what does deconstruction as a method, portend for literary criticism which in one way or another has to embrace all the assumptions of an aesthetic that is part and parcel metaphysical, an aesthetic that assumes the indissoluble relation between poetry and truth, and thus privileges form, consciousness, and even poetic language itself? In one way or another, literature is considered a metaphor for or of truth, of meaning or sense, or is inflated into the kerygmatic utterance of the single word which metaphysical thinking in one way or another pursues as its lost origin.

Geoffrey Hartman has posed the desperate question (or is it a plea?) for the humanist "crisis" of our time: "Is it too late, or can our age, like every previous one, protect the concept of art?"[2] Art, of course, is a "concept" and as such takes its meaning within the horizon of the very metaphysics which is under attack by those who would save art from metaphysics. The fact that Hartman's question is posed most desperately in the face of the "baroquely elaborated asceticism of the School of Derrida" is revealing, for it is a plea to maintain the fiction of self-presencing even in the face of a questioning that forces him to recognize that the fiction is itself a simulacrum. Hartman's plea may sound Heideggerean in urging a return to "wonder" and therefore to an authentic art that will preserve us against an inauthentic, ascetic, deconstructive thought. And it may well share something with the early Heidegger, though with a difference which is of no point here. Heidegger surely does make a last, late defense of the concept of art, displacing as it were the classical conception of representation (which Hartman, following his master Auerbach, has reappropriated) with another (presencing), but in no way moving beyond the implication of art in the concept of presence.

Is Derrida, then, the great disenchanter, who in making a game of the concept has placed the concept *hors jeu?* that is, declared it offside? Has Derrida's disruption of the "play of language"—which Heidegger so eloquently proclaims as "bound to the hidden rule"[3] that commands the reciprocal difference of poetry and thinking and thus governs *aletheia*—has Derrida's "play," by revealing the "hidden rule" as the law of all metaphoricity, destroyed the concept of art and perhaps given us back "literature" (again, in quotation marks)? In a way (not Heideggerean) this essay will concern itself with the different paths broken by this figure of language's play in Heidegger and Derrida, since it is within the parentheses of these names that the future of the metaphor "poetic language" turns.

II

Even for the literary critic, the basic Heidegger text remains *Being and Time*,[4] appropriately incomplete, almost a pre-text to a writing that would appear in another, fragmentary form, primarily as lectures or essays. *Being and Time* is in a sense a clearing of obstacles (classical ontology) in a path that will lead to language—a methodology which destroys by overcoming, that is, reappropriating. But it has turned up in literary criticism in a number of ways indifferent to its methodology: as an existential analytic, as a text of modern thematics, with its identification of care, anxiety, fallenness, being-toward-death, being-in-the-world, and so on, the themes, in short, of a phenomenology. Its method, however, has tended to undermine thematics, which is always tied to the ontology against which the book was directed. Thus Heidegger begins with a hermeneutic already situated within a tradition of conceptualization, and proposes to clear that history as a way of gaining access to the "primordial 'sources' from which the categories and concepts handed down to us have been in part genuinely drawn" (BT, 43). His delineation of a method which will "destroy the traditional content of ancient ontology" (BT, 44) proceeds through the matrix of a philosophical metaphoricity that presents itself as a content. It is an exercise in language, in translation, an etymological unweaving that finally comes to the point of declaring its own theme as the problematics of language.

As Heidegger protested in later texts, the destructive hermeneutic was easily misinterpreted as a kind of etymological retreat in search of the archaic origin of conceptuality and even for the origin of language (see QB, 93, where he says that, despite numerous misinterpretations, the "destruction" did not "desire to win back the original experiences of metaphysics"). The clearing projected a reappropriation, not a philological archaism. The development of what would later become the poetics of Being, of the metaphysical forgetting of Being as the unconcealed, of *logos* as the reciprocal difference of *physis*, of the Same that marks the difference between thinking and saying, does seem implicit in the destruction. Certainly the figure of "breaking" a "path," of opening the "way" to language, and therefore of achieving an "authentic" language or "articulating" the "proximity" of Being and being, is anticipated by a destruction which no more advocates a return to some ideal or primordial philosophizing than it suggests a full recuperation of some lost essence or truth. Heidegger's early discourse on his method locates his search clearly within the temporal horizon of Dasein, and thus within the "limits" of interpretation.

The theme of language emerges rather late in the first section of *Being and Time*, and then as language in general, or more accurately, as the speech or discourse of "interpretation" through which Dasein discloses itself. The interpretation of Greek ontology uncovers the definition of Dasein as that "living thing whose Being is essentially determined by the potentiality for discourse" (BT, 47). Language as such becomes the relation of the temporal unfolding of the Being of Dasein. Thus when Heidegger finally arrives at language as "theme" (BT, 203), he must preoccupy himself largely with a destruction of the concept of language as the deposited understanding of historical knowledge (*Garede* or "idle talk"). But he reserves the privileged concept of speech or discourse as the structure of Dasein. As

Derrida reveals in a reading of Heidegger's famous footnote on time (see BT, 500), this early Heideggerean separation of the authentic and inauthentic, of the primordial and the derivative, of discourse as the structure of the Being of Dasein and "idle talk," of *Verfallen* as the passage from one temporality to the other, constitutes a reappropriation of metaphysics: "Is there not at least some Platonism in the notion of *Verfallen*...?"[5] If the "destruction" suspends nostalgia and repudiates the dream of some recovery of archaic concepts, it produces on the other side of nostalgia the figure of the potential return of presence, a figure that always effaces itself, producing in Heidegger a kind of metaphysical "hope," the "quest for the proper word and the unique name" (*Margins*, p. 27). The destructive method of *Being and Time* employs a hermeneutical violence or a systematic interrogation of the onto-theological concepts which reside within and govern the structure of Western thought: particularly the concepts that define the relation between Being and beings. Thus the crucial concept of time. This interrogation differs from understanding, as Heidegger presents it in Section 32 of *Being and Time* (pp. 188 ff.), in the sense of a development that overthrows the concept of understanding. The development is disruptive—a disruption of any significance that may be presumed to inhere in the already interpreted (the present-at-hand), and thus disruptive of the habit of imposing significance upon the present as if that significance were immanent in the thing. Interpretation as reappropriation is grounded in understanding, but always goes beyond it, breaking the interpreted free from its circumspect context of involvements. Interpretation always involves a putting in question and the assumption of a point of view (not in this case subjective). The displacement effected in interpretation is a kind of "articulation," an assertion that communicates, and thus a retelling that is shared with others (sometimes viewed as a theory of intersubjectivity). Interpretation is therefore grounded in what Heidegger calls "fore-having" (*Vorhabe*, or "what is before us" or "what we have in advance"), "foresight" (*Vorsicht*, or "what we see in advance"), and "foreconception" (*Vorgriff*, or anticipation, "what we grasp in advance"). This Heideggerean foreplay as anticipation disrupts the concept of the a priori. It presents the present-at-hand to be interpreted as the already interpreted, as already appropriated in the structure of discourse that is at the same time originary and forestructured. Language is always involved in interpretation, in an always incomplete disclosure.

For literary criticism this projection of "foreknowledge" may be the literary text itself. This text is situated in a context, a language within language, a text which is at the same time concealed and unconcealed, an interpretation demanding interpretation. Every interpretation already presumes a meaning (or "operates in the forestructure," as Heidegger writes), but more significantly, it presumes a point (a proximity) between the concealed knowledge of the text and that knowledge which interpretation can disclose: "Any interpretation which is to contribute understanding, must already have understood what is to be interpreted" (BT, 194).

Heidegger's hermeneutic circle, however, is not a vicious circle, not closed. It is a circle that in its approximation of closure allows the text to become fully disclosed, though such an ideal disclosure would also lead to a disappearance or effacement of the text as a forestructure. Thus the hermeneutic circle, though inescapable, is liberating. It embraces the limitations of the "existential constitution of Dasein" (BT, 195). "What is decisive," Heidegger writes, "is not to get out of the circle but to come into it the right way," by a deliberate process of determining the forestructure. For once the circle is defined as the potential for interpretation, we discover that it hides within itself a "positive possibility of the most primordial kind of knowing" (BT, 195). But the possibility of a full disclosure, or an ideal commentary, is already denied. Interpretation bears within its structure an always deferred end.

At the point in *Being and Time* where assertion as predication and communication becomes the way of "methodological foresight," Heidegger introduces language as his "theme *for the first time*" (BT, 203), language "which already hides in itself a developed way of conceiving" (BT, 199). Language here is the structure of Dasein, and not yet, as it will become, the "house of Being," poetic language. But even here, language as discourse is identified with the presencing of speech and not the secondariness of writing: "*The existential-ontological foundation of language is discourse or talk*" (BT, 203). Talk as communication is always about something, but this something is not simply a thing explained or defined: "What the discourse is about is a structural item that it necessarily possesses, and its own structure is modelled upon this basic state of Dasein" (BT, 205). Language is the structure of Man. (At this point in the text, page 202, Heidegger projects that the full development of the question of Being will appear in a later section, which in fact he never wrote, except in the form of the later fragments, essays, and lectures on language as the "house of Being.") But language is not the ontological structure of man as subject. As Heidegger indicates in the "Letter on Humanism," the proximity of man and language confirms the proximity (nearness) of man and Being, not in the sense of two existences but in the sense of their sharing the same structure of presencing. In *Being and Time*, however, the particular nature of poetic language is defined as a very special form of communication: "In 'poetical' discourse, the communication of the existential possibilities of one's state-of-mind can become an aim in itself, and this amounts to a disclosing of existence" (BT, 205).

The seeds of a phenomenological poetics lie within this kind of possibility, though "state-of-mind" here is not pure consciousness or cogito, but a consciousness of consciousness, an interpretation of consciousness as projected in the structure of language. In the later Heidegger, poetry will become the purest mode of its own interpretation because as the primal form of discourse or talk it is a disclosure of the "structural item that it necessarily possesses." The destruction of metaphysics, then, clears the way for the later meditations on the "way to language," by a discourse that reveals the structure hidden within "idle talk" or received historical understanding. As a method, the destruction can only be the reverse form of the later interpretation of poetry or authentic language, since as an interpretation of the inauthentic it is an interpretation of the world as text, as fallenness, the world as already interpreted. The destruction makes way for thinking, and for a kind of interpretative commentary which is reciprocal with the saying of poetry, with poetry as originary naming.

It is the status of the language of Being, or language which situates the nearness of man and Being, that has been the object of Derrida's most severe questioning. (As he puts it in "The Ends of Man," this proximity does not mark the relation between two ontological beings but between the sense of being and the sense of man—a kind of security that is displaced by a thinking that announces the end of man to be implicit in the language of Being—*Margins*, 114–17.) And ironically, as Heidegger has moved more and more toward the prophetic and oracular celebration of a poetic language as the "house of Being," and man as the "shepherd of Being," Dasein has tended to be displaced, and with him the structural model of discourse as communication. Heidegger's later method, fully embracing poetic language as originary speech, has become increasingly less useful for literary criticism. Paul de Man has been one of the subtlest interpreters of Heideggerean hermeneutics for American criticism, arguing for the privilege, the authenticity, of poetic language. But he stops short of embracing the "prophetic poeticism" of the later Heidegger.[6] Instead, he begins with Heidegger's highlighting the positive possibility of reaching a primordial kind of knowledge, hidden within language, and derives from it a view of the irreducible doubleness of literary language which he can accommodate to even the most severe poststructuralist critiques of Heidegger.

De Man's interpretation of literary language as that which forever names the void lying between sign and meaning derives from Heidegger's non-expressive view of a discourse that names the "existential possibilities of one's state of mind," in the sense that it always names the difference of understanding, of mediation. Thus literature, for de Man, always names itself as fiction. It is the foreknowledge of our understanding of the special nature of language. For de Man as for Heidegger, literary language is never self-deceived about the problematic that opens between the word and the thing; though unlike Heidegger, de Man will not prefigure what literary language does name, the void, as the site of an emerging truth. De Man is a negative Heideggerean, like Maurice Blanchot. The privileging of literary language for de Man is not derived from its power of unconcealing but lies in its resistance to self-mystification, its refusal to name presence, and its repeated naming of distance that is "nothing." For de Man there is the void rather than proximity or the site. The authenticity of literary language lies in its persistent naming of itself as fiction, and thus of its unique double function as the origin of the self and the naming of the self's nothingness, the naming of the subject as a necessary function.

III

De Man, then, begins as a critic of consciousness intent on putting that criticism within definite parentheses, marking the limits which govern the strengths of the phenomenological critique. For de Man there can be an authentic criticism as well as an authentic literature, so long as that criticism is oriented toward the literary text as a kind of foreknowledge, as a totalized understanding of the absolute fissure between language and what it is presumed to name or to disclose. Inauthentic criticism, on the other hand, idealizes or mystifies poetry. And Heidegger's late "prophetic poeticism" is for him a form of this self-mystification. De Man's reappropriation of Heidegger is not offered here simply as one form of American mistranslation, but because it points up some of the possible directions criticism takes from Heidegger's overthrowing of metaphysics. But de Man's interpretation of literary language as authentic does not derive solely from *Being and Time*; it comes as much by way of some intermediary texts. Both Blanchot's and de Man's hermeneutics move by way of the insertion of the "nothing" into the Heideggerean critique, the "nothing" of "What Is Metaphysics?" which is conceived as the "pure 'Other'" and as the "veil of Being." Heidegger's own philosophical "turn" (*Kehre*) from language as the structure of Dasein to language as the "house of Being" depends on his thought of the abyss and thus on the thought of "nothing" as a productive principle.

The consequences of these thoughts for Heidegger's conception of the nature of language is revealed in another early lecture, "The Origin of the Work of Art" (first read in 1935),[7] a deconstruction of the concept of aesthetics as it is implicated in classical ontology. Though a bridge to the later thinking of po-

etry as the presencing of presence, the essay has not yet
adopted the full-throated kerygmatic tones of the later meditations, perhaps because the essay's concern is as much with the
"work" as "thing" as with the problem of origins. Still, Heidegger's ultimate concern is with art as truth (*aletheia*). Therefore,
the opening of Being through language, while set against the
metaphysical concept of the subject as origin and so against all
theories of art as expression or representation, is presented as a
metaphorical "rift." This is not the basic dualism of a subject become exterior, or an idea fallen into form, but the double nature of unconcealedness. Metaphorically, Heidegger presents
this rift as between "earth" and "world," between the closed and
the open, opposites always in conflict, reciprocal differences:
"Truth is un-truth, insofar as there belongs to it the reservoir of
the not-yet-uncovered, the un-covered, in the sense of conceal-
ment. In unconcealedness, as truth, there occurs also the other
'un-' of a double restraint or refusal. Truth occurs as such in
the opposition of clearing and double concealing" (PLT, 60).
One recalls the figural "place" of the poet in the Holderlin essays, situated in the time of the "double-Not" (need) of the old
gods who have disappeared and the new ones who have not yet
come.

The rift is a "between" that is a "measure." The conflictual situation of "earth" and "world," which seems to anticipate the
later redefinitions of *physis* and *logos*, is a figural place—the
place as figure, the figure as place. "Createdness of the work
means: truth's being fixed in place of the fiqure. Figure is the
structure in whose shape the rift composes and submits itself"
(PLT, 64). In the later essays, this place of poetry's opening will
be presented figurally (as the "house of Being" or "bourne of
Being," etc.), but a figure that is already doubly effaced and
rendered as the Being of language (beyond metaphor). In this
essay, the figure is double-faced, a Gestalt, a form of writing.
Thus Heidegger opens up the possibility of a figural analysis in
which the rift of the figure is the nothing it names, the distance
between sign and meaning. But in Heidegger the figure is the
appearance, as opposed to the expression, of truth. Language
now appears as something other than the vehicle of communication: "Language is not only and not primarily an audible and

written expression of what is to be communicated. It not only puts forth in words and statements what is overtly or covertly intended to be communicated; language alone brings what is, as something that is, into the Open for the first time" (PLT, 73). Thus the reification of poetry as "inaugural naming."

In the same gesture, language for Heidegger is turned into a figure for some primal signification: "Language is not poetry because it is primal poesy" (PLT, 74). That is, poetry is the secondary sign, words, in which a primary language, poesy, takes its place. The primal is not the primitive but the originating. Art is historical for Heidegger in the sense that it reinvents the beginning of history as an opening. It is an appropriation and an overthrowing of the historical, and thus an original beginning (origin as *Ursprung* or "primal leap"). Poetic language overthrows "actual language," of which it is the origin, yet in its appearance it doubly effaces itself. Poetic language cannot be analyzed and criticized as a system of signs, but only prompted to bespeak itself. Veiled in a figural shape that has already disrupted the metaphoricity of actual language, it speaks of Being as at once inside and outside of metaphor. It introduces us to a history that holds out the hope for some full recovery of presence, some evocation of the first word of Being.

Poetic language, then, portends a text that overthrows its own temporality. (Poetic) language is a metaphor of that which is the author of all metaphor, the non-metaphoric Being. It is the "first word" without which the origin of language, Being, could not have its Being. Thus Being must also be metaphoric, already inscribed in the system as the name of the origin of the system—a system in Heidegger's case that fully declares itself as language. Heidegger admits to the "mystery of language" that "admits to two things": "One, that it be reduced to a mere system of signs, uniformly available to everybody . . . ; and two, that language at one great moment says one unique thing, for one time only, which remains inexhaustible because it is ordinary" (WICT, 191–92).[8] The first recalls the "idle talk" of *Being and Time*, or "actual language," but even these signs do not submit to the materiality of linguistic description. Both written language and acoustical sounds are for him abstractions. Words are "well-springs" (WICT, 130), and they can be named only metaphorically. They must be repeatedly "dug up." Thus poetic language is the excavation of language by language.

This operation, the gift of Being, can only be accomplished metaphorically: one can only dig in a "place." Things only bloom in a "field": "the saying [of poetic utterance or authentic thinking] *speaks* where there are no words, in the field between words" (WICT, 186). The remark comes in regard to a commentary on a text of Parmenides, and emphasizes the paratactic grammar of this pre-Socratic style of thinking, including the significance of the graphic sign of punctuation, the colon. But contrary to the reading of such signs in modern linguistics or grammatology, Heidegger reads them as figural measures of a saying which speaks in silence. Thinking and saying *speak* in a place marked by the sign, but they speak a proper word to which words are related as Being is related (or articulated) to beings. Writing, or script, on the other hand, is for Heidegger a near total repression of the saying of speech. On Nietzsche and the sometime need to resort to writing, Heidegger characterizes the Nietzschean style as a generative violence directed against philosophical writing. If originary saying is related to speech, a response to some "call" or "appeal," there are occasions, says Heidegger, when only a "scream" will answer the "call." But the "scream" is difficult to achieve in writing:

> Script easily smothers the scream, especially if the script exhausts itself in description, and aims to keep men's imaginations busy by supplying it constantly with new matter. The burden of thought is swallowed up in the written script, unless the writing is capable of remaining, even in the script itself, a progress of thinking, a way. (WICT, 49)

The privileging of speech over writing (speech as presenting-saying and not speech as acoustic sign, another form of writing) is persistent and massive in Heidegger, and is consistent with the valorization of presence which entangles him in the very metaphysical network he has so methodically overthrown and announced as ended. (Derrida marks this as the difference between the closure of metaphysics and the end of philosophy, as Heidegger announces the latter in his book on Nietzsche.) More of this later. But at this point it is necessary to consider the consequences for literary criticism of the suppression of the text explicit in Heidegger's view of (poetic) language. Quite obviously the idea of a text has always included not only the idea of totalization but also the economy of the signifier—the text not only as scripted writing, as Derrida says, but as a "re-mark," a re-inscription of a previous discourse and its conceptualization. Text is therefore itself a metaphor for a totalization of elements which reveals itself as a metaphor of this totality. For Heidegger, poetry or even literature cannot be this kind of re-marking, since it is original, the original speech of the (not-yet-disclosed) "proper word."

"Script," which smothers the "scream," is for Heidegger a kind of second-order language, representational, unless the style can overcome itself. Heidegger's example of Nietzschean writing which overcomes the script is an "aphorism," the writing of a poetic utterance which overthrows sense or ordinary understanding. The writing-speech of aphorism is therefore the utterance of the "one thought" that every true thinker repeatedly thinks, or the "one unique thing" that authentic language says "at one great moment" (WICT, 191). It is not rhetoric. Like the "single poetic statement" which at once rises from and remains concealed in the site (as source) of every poet's saying, and "always remains in the realm of the unspoken,"[9] (poetic) language is a silence which speaks Being but has no being. The source of metaphor, the site of figure, it is non-figural. And its origin is natural, in the sense of *physis*. The poetic text, then, is only a kind of veil, or the rhythm of a passage, a trace of Being, a metaphoric detour which at the same time turns the thinker of the text toward the site and prevents his looking directly into its full light. (Poetic) language cannot be destroyed, or appropriated, in the sense of overthrowing the metaphysical concept; any interrogation of it must take the form of a dialogue, a "poetic dialogue," that emerges in the "reciprocity between discussion and clarification" (OWTL, 160). There is an authentic criticism, then, or an ideal commentary as de Man says, already posited in Heidegger's early writing, that emerges as a proximal possibility in his later work. If poets think the holy, the true dialogue would be like a conversation between poets. On the other hand, there is the dialogue between thinking and poetry (as saying), or between two different kinds of discourse which share a "proper" relation to language. But even in the conflict-ual reciprocity of this dialogue, Heidegger returns to the cau-tion of the Holderlin essays, that the critical statement must open a way to the pure utterance of the poem and in that act annihilate itself, or become the silence of the "unique word": "in order that what has been purely written of in the poem may stand forth a little clearer, the explanatory speech must break up each time both itself and what it has attempted. The final, but at the same time the most difficult, step of every exposition consists in vanishing away together with its explanation in the face of the pure existence of the poem," allowing the poem to "throw light directly on the other poems" (EB, 234–35).[10]

Taken as a description of the critical discourse, this kind of statement might point toward a criticism which begins with in-dividual poems but evolves into a study of the unitary metaphorics of the poetic canon, a criticism of consciousness as the exploration of one poet's site. But this figural site is the site of all authentic poets, the site of poetry itself. Commentary, Heidegger writes, should ultimately sound like the "fall of snow on the bell" (EB, 234), a figure derived from Holderlin, from authentic language. In the poetic fragment from which it is drawn, the metaphor of snow falling on bell is a figure of disso-nance, of that which smothers the "tune" of the bell which calls one to meals, to sustenance. Heidegger's deployment of this figure appears in a "Prefatory Remark to a Repetition of the Ad-dress," itself an explanation of his own repeated smothering of the pure self-interpretation of poetic language, and is thus a forestructuring of his own lecture as that which will vanish in his utterance, remembering the poet in the silence of its own end. Heidegger's essays on poets and poetry regularly end in the poet's words, with the poem which is the first and last word. Heidegger's dialogue with Holderlin turns out to be an effort in self-annihilating thinking, an apology for the reappropria-tion of pure saying in the explanation which transcribes, trans-lates, and transgresses poetic language, turning it into its other. Thus Heidegger's Preface turns his afterword into a foreword that forewarns of its own dulling of the pure tones of the holy.

It marks off the critical text as a bypath to the poetry which has already explored the bypath of poetic homecoming.

The Preface, then, repeats the essay's own theme of incompleteness, of the poetic deferral of the naming of the holy. It repeats for us the poet's theme of poetic foreknowledge: "his knowledge of the mystery of the reserving proximity" (EB, 269). This site of proximity or place of mystery is the place of the "double-Not" (EB, 289). The mystery is not revealed by the poet, but is only protected. This mystery as "reserving proximity" is the mystery of language, its generative power or Being, that must be protected from writing. The poet, whose singing still lacks the proper word or "naming word," offers a "song without words," a song which holds open, by deferring, the end in which the others (the non-poets) may also have their homecoming, the ultimate understanding of the proper word. As Heidegger interprets Holderlin, the poet protects the "reserving proximity" so that the others, those "of writing *and* of thinking," may always be directed towards the true source of language and not be sidetracked by its historical misadventures. The poet protects the mystery by calling to the others, by calling their thinking to his saying, thus remembering the community of man.

IV

Derrida's critique of Heidegger's metaphorics takes not only the form of systematic questioning, but in itself consists of a methodological doubling of the destruction, a strategy which must go beyond the fundamental inversion of basic concepts and mark a divergence which will prevent the conceptual reappropriation of those same concepts. Derrida finds the Heideggerean error to lie in this destruction that inverts and reappropriates, thus overthrowing metaphysics and reinscribing it fully within the thinking of presence. Heidegger presents a problem for Derrida at every turn. He has been the subject of two essays in particular, but the name reverberates everywhere in the Derridean canon, as an example of the problematics involved in any metaphysical reappropriation or in any overthrow of metaphysics, not the least being the inflation of language and the relation between literature and truth in Heideggerean thinking.

Derrida never underplays the difficulty of reading Heidegger, nor ignores the implications of turning a methodology against itself, of deconstructing the deconstructor. One might say, then, that Derrida *underwrites* Heidegger, in the various and contradictory senses of that word: to place the thinking of presence in italics, to become a signatory to the difference, to re-mark the metaphysical implications of writing an end to metaphysics, to submit Heidegger's valorization of speech to the mark of a *proto-écriture* which it tries to conceal, etc. Derrida's relentless questioning of the metaphysical hierarchy which places speech in a privileged relation to presence, and reduces writing to a secondary function, is literally an *underwriting* of the idea of a poetic language, of language that claims to escape the double sense of the metaphoric.

In "Différance," Derrida submits the Heideggerean text, "Der Spruch des Anaximander," to an extensive deconstruction, concentrating on the Heideggerean language of presence and the difference "between pre*sence* and pre*sent*" (*Margins*, 23–27). The thrust of the Derridean critique inserts a double mark into Heidegger's attack on metaphysics which has, as Heidegger notes, "forgotten" the difference between Being and beings. Derrida submits the Heideggerean figure of the "trace" of the difference, which must be effaced in the appearance of being-present to an irruptive discourse. What Heidegger calls the "matinal trace" of the difference which effaces itself in the moment of Being's appearance, in order that Being might maintain its essence or its difference from beings, is also a figure analogous to what he calls the "mystery" of poetic language: the "difference between Being and beings" can be forgotten only if it "has left a trace which remains preserved in the language which to which Being comes" (quoted in *Margins*, 23–25). Derrida's questioning of this trace traces it to its source in another language. In repeating the Heideggerean step, he disrupts the Heideggerean way. The trace as "sustaining use" is a simulacrum of the name of Being, and not the appearance of the difference itself.

In this classic act of deconstruction, Derrida interrupts the Heideggerean text in order to reveal that Heidegger's deployment of the concept difference reappropriates the metaphysical text it seems to disrupt. In the same gesture, Derrida disrupts the thinking of hierarchical difference. "There is no essence of difference," he writes, and thus no trace or name for it that is not already a metaphysical inscription or another trace, the trace of a trace. Thus Derrida, who has already coined the name "différance" as a trace of the concept difference which turns out to be a trace, a trace which has already effaced itself, provides a model of a critique which resists the reappropriation of the concept through inversion; he re-marks the divergence of a name that is not a word, not a concept, though it may stimulate the concept (which is already a trace). Rather than examining a text for its unconcealed sense, or for its thematic differences which trace a hidden unity or promise a recovered word, Derrida inserts another language into the text, in order to reveal that the "text" is composed of different orders of signs and not signs which trace a single sense. The language of différance under*writes* the concept difference and renders it a simulacrum or undecidable. It names the *name* of the difference, the word which is the name for all the possible substitutions for any of the commanding or privileged concepts which might govern the differences of the text—whereas Heidegger sees the metaphysical forgetting of the difference to be the determining movement of Being, and can thus promise in his own text that which is always deferred in his interrogations of language, the ultimate overcoming of the difference of Being and being in the "proper name." But as Derrida concludes, the writing of différance reveals that there never was a "proper name" but only the unnameable play that produces "nominal effects," just as "the false entry or false exit is still part of the game" (*Margins*, 27).

Now, it is not so much this interrogation of Heidegger which should instruct us here, as it is the Derridean thinking of textuality itself—though in this particular case, Derrida's critique of the Heideggerean "language of Being" is also a critique of the authenticity of poetic speech. If poets are, as Heidegger writes in "The Origin of the Work of Art," those who "sense the trace of the fugitive gods" and thus trace the realm of the holy, they provide only traces of traces, and thus protect the mystery of the source (PLT, 94). "Language," which "is not poetry because it is primal poesy," is itself only a trace, a figural play of irreducible differences. Thus the expanding network of Heideggerean figures for present and presencing—site, house, bridge, etc.—might be analyzed as metaphorical traces of a word that is always already metaphorical, the name of the origin, the name that is already inscribed in every system as the center. Language, for Heidegger, is the name of Being as presence, the name of naming. Language not only "gathers" the two-fold—it is an already doubled metaphor. Heidegger features the double function of the *present* participle, at once noun and verb, as the temporal naming of Being—gathering, thinging, thinking, saying, bridging, dwelling, building, showing, relating, blooming, etc.

In *The Question of Being,* Heidegger speaks of authentic language as a "meaning-fullness." Its plenitude of sense is not an historical accumulation, but a play of unfolding, a "play which, the more richly it unfolds, the more strictly it is bound by the hidden rules" (QB, 105). The play of meaning is always commanded by an origin it can never fully name. The "meaning-fullness" of the word is determined by a rule that is fuller than meaning, by Being which appropriates that which in every appearance leaves it behind in bringing it to light. This is a play easily comprehended with the tradition in which we measure the depth of the work of art, a fathomless, resourceful text which interpretation can never exhaust. Derrida, on the other hand, inserts into the thinking of the text and interpretation a more playful figure of play, in which the production of meanings turns upon a meaninglessness, an absence of the commanding, originating word, and the play of the *supplément* which stands for that word (that center) in the text. In doing so, Derrida deprives us of literature in its relation to truth, only to give us back literature already in quotation marks, a text whose meaningfulness resides in its play of differences. Criticism begins with an insertion of a question into the opening provided by the text, into the double sense of the operative signifier; an operation which often consists of raising the illusory governing concept or "proper word" from the text in order to re-mark it, to mark its double sense and doubling function, and to trace its itinerary as a simulacrum. Thus Derrida's own (non-)concepts: *trace, différance, supplement, pharmakon, dissemination, écart, hymen, grammē*, etc., which he calls "undecidables" or "simulacra," words and concepts that are only the semantic mirage of real words and concepts, as if there were real words and concepts.

As examples, we might point to the two complementary essays, "White Mythology" (in *Margins*, 207–72) and "The Double Session,"[11] both deconstructions of the Heideggerean principle of thinking and saying. "White Mythology" is a rigorous interrogation of metaphor in philosophy; "The Double Session" is a systematic disruption of the idea of literature as truth, either as representation or as *aletheia*, at once a diruptive reading of an imaginative text (Mallarmé's *Mimique*) and of idealized or totalized readings of that text. Derrida's strategy is to approach one text through another, whether the second text is a reading of the first or not. The indirection or detour is consistent with the nature of all textuality—that is, a text is never self-sufficient or self-present, never in itself a totalization of meaning or a concealment/unconcealment of a unitary sense. "White Mythology" introduces the problematics of philosophical language through the imaginary dialogue of a literary or fictional text (by Anatole France), itself already a kind of parody of the philosophical dialogue. "The Double Session" opens in the field between a philosophical (Platonic) and an imaginative (Mallarmean) text, texts that in their way mark the opening and closing of metaphysics and in which is posed the question of the absolute reciprocal difference between two modes of truth. This involves Derrida in an examination of various rhetorical strategies—including the placement and function of operational elements, both verbal and non-verbal, in the text, the deployment of the title, the use of the epigraph, the function of grammatological marks.

The central text of "The Double Session" is Mallarmé's, the title of which already provides a *capital* instance of the question of representation and "what is represented?" But Derrida does not submit the work of literature to criticism. His reading is a re-marking of the text within other readings of it, in particular the impressive book of J. P. Richard which incorporates the coherent thematic play of this one Mallarmé work into a totalized reading of the Mallarmé canon as an imaginary world: a world or unity evident in the intricate play of thematic differences that dialectically unfold and enfold the unity of consciousness or imagination. For Derrida, such readings of the thematic or semantic richness of a work only reveal that the depth of the text is a semantic mirage generated by the play of heterogeneous signifiers which refuse to be commanded by any single element within (meaning) or without (author) the text. Thus Derrida deconstructs Richard's and other critical readings of Mallarmé by raising the textual undecidable, the "hymen," from its thematic role in order to show how it works as a grammatological function to disrupt the concept of mimesis named in the title and already displaced as an initiatory key to the text. It functions as a mark, as a slash (/), and as a title with two faces. It functions always to disrupt the positioning of any representation that is not itself a representation of a representation. Thus it functions to upset the illusion that there can be truth in literature, or the appearance of an unrepresented in the represented, the concealed which is unconcealed yet hidden.

There is nothing represented that is not already a representation, just as in "White Mythology" there is no pure or natural origin of metaphor which stands behind or beneath the play of traces, but only metaphorical play itself. Derrida's strategic re-marking of concepts, by a forceful inversion followed by, as he says, a divergence, is necessary to keep his own undecidables in play, and to resist the overpowering tendency of the names to be reconceptualized. Thus Derrida's artful footwork of renaming his "positions" so as to avoid that any one of his names falls into a position of initiatory concept: most obviously, the undecidable *écriture* which many critics of Derrida have tried to locate as his privileged position. All of his undecidables recall, like a distant echo or a veiled shape, some etymological legacy which they at the same time *underwrite*, trace, and efface. Thus

the conflictual nature of the Derridean text inverts the Heideggerean conflict, and diverges from it; Derrida's gap or break or
hymen redoubles Heidegger's rift; his dissemination disrupts
Heideggerean flowering.

Écriture is not the name for the physical mark of writing, but
the doubleness of which the physical mark is always a sign—a
sign that has no signified except another sign. Thus the productive function of *écriture* which, like *différance*, initiates by an
instant replay. The limitlessness of literature is not the concealed fullness of language, but its disruptive and temporalizing
function. "Literature" is neither a full text nor an empty text,
neither a presence nor an absence. There is no literary language, not even in de Man's sense, for there can be no privileged language. Derrida's critique disrupts the classical play of
difference which always begins or ends with one of the two
terms in a position of authority. Literature can be privileged,
then, only because it is the purest function of the self-dissimu-
lating movement of writing. Literature is writing—the figure of
a productive function for which the produced text is only a simulacrum, a facsimile, a factor. The literary text is a play of textuality, not simply in the obvious sense that a work of art always
originates in the historical field of predecessors. Its own play of
differences mirrors its displacement and reappropriation of
other texts, and anticipates the necessary critical text that must
supplement it, insert into it the undecidable or raise the undecidable which is dissimulated in it as a unique word. The Derridean rhetoric names the double-play of chance as the (non-)
law of literature. Thus Derrida threatens to disrupt the whole
cultural order which has given literature a "place" at the center
because it could assume that literature was the *arche* and *eidos* of
order. But then, he gives us back literature as the double-name
of man, who makes metaphor, who interprets.

Derrida is a kind of Dupin, a decipherer in pursuit of a letter
which is always moving, always displaced, always doubled, always
at hand and underhanded, an author who is already only the
sign of another (pre)text. Dupin, who, through the distracting
ruse of some "pretended lunatic," reappropriates the letter and
replaces it with that which appears externally as a *"fac-simile,"*
but on the inside is a sign reappropriated from literature, mark-

ing its transgressions. Dupin who is the double of the narrator, shares the sign ("D——") of the thief, and is the double-name of author-interpreter-seducer, who cannot *write* either a beginning or end to literature, who cannot escape the circuit of the sign as the "factoring" of a "truth" that never gets outside "literature," and is never fully delivered.

Chapter Two
H.D. and Freud

I

Freud locates the beginning of analysis (might we extend it to literary criticism? even poetry?) in the legendary problematic of Moses's stutter; that is, in the necessity for translation, but a translation that can never quite correct a textual distortion it aggravates. In that curious reconstruction of a certain history that became his own allegory of modern crisis, *Moses and Monotheism,* Freud provides history itself with a decisive origin, by excavating what has been forgotten and/or repressed.[1] His reconstruction, however, has the effect of doubling and retextualizing the origin, implicating it in the question mark of all writing, in the cursive traces of the alphabet. We are not, here, at the beginning of culture, but at the "moment" of cultural dispersal, or its division of a division, where in the Freudian projection, the polytheistic and monotheistic families have their origins in the tangle of a father whose role is always more decisive than clear. In the Freudian history, polytheistic culture is characterized by "hieroglyphic picture writing" and monotheism by the problematic of representation signified by a prohibition of images or representations of the deity. Hence monotheism is allied with a history of phonetic writing, the fixation by writing of an event that is itself already an interpretation, maintained in the oral tradition. This text, which has displaced an event only to reveal its irreducible textuality, is never the hand of a single author, but is already a diacritical text. And though Freud is addressing here the particular texts that make up the "history of King David" and the "scribes of

Moses," what he has to say locates the origin in a text that has no depth but two faces: "Two mutually opposed treatments have left their traces on it" (XIII, 43).

The two "treatments" (another translation might be "forces") characterize a surface of a palimpsest, or a multiple of surfaces, that make up the illusion of depth: the one working a transformation which falsifies the text (itself already a transcription) in accord with "secret aims," the other anxious to conserve the mystery of the text's original relation with the event. The two effect a distortion, simultaneously grounding and erasing the ground of the text. Thus Freud's remarkable elision of historical textuality and dream-work:

> Thus almost everywhere noticeable gaps, disturbing repetitions and obvious contradictions have come about—indications which reveal things to us which it was not intended to communicate. In its implications, the distortion of a text resembles a murder: the difficulty lies not in perpetrating the deed, but in getting rid of its traces. We might well lend the word "*Entstellung* [distortion]" the double meaning to which it has a claim but of which to-day it makes no use. It should mean not only "to change the appearance of something" but also "to put something in another place, to displace." Accordingly, in many instances of textual distortion, we may nevertheless count upon finding what has been suppressed and disavowed hidden away somewhere else, though changed and torn from its context. (XIII, 43)

The question of textuality is inextricable from the Oedipal crossing, from a murder whose traces will not be erased but which are never anything more than traces of other distortions. Freud's text is already allegorized in his writings as the "family romance," and therefore already marked by the double face: (1) Is it the interpretation of an event or (2) an interpretation of interpretation? A murder in two senses? Is it the clarification of a tangle and the re-inscription of it? A complex?! Or an image that is neither a pictorial representation nor an abstract description, but a weave of two diametrically opposed kinds of writing? The family romance is an analytical machine which can never be extricated from nor given priority to the subject matter it allegedly addresses or represents. This distortion, then, cannot be the sole product of the analytical text, or the translation, but is integral to the very notion of a primary text—

whether that primary text is thought of as poetic (literary) or historical. What we call modern or even Romantic literature has been the cunning recuperation of an analysis that has always been marked in literature as the Oedipal crossroads, the scene of interpretation that is not only a murder but a strategically shoddy covering up of its traces. This crossing has taken the place of the origin, proving finally to be the only mark of origin—the sign of the beginning as distortion or maiming, and of writing as a strange, wayward walking, or as the bridging of an abyss that indelibly marks the abyss as the vertiginous meaning. A chiasmus signifying a catachresis.

Pound's theory of the Image was in itself a kind of anti-logos or literary machine, producing and disseminating in the fictions of stylistic objectivity and *mot juste* a theory of translation as creative distortion, a double writing. If the primordial text or event is already literary, already cultural (an interpretation) and not natural, literature is never at the origin, nor even proximate to a nature, but the text in which nature appears. Nature as presence, therefore, does not precede what properly represents its appearance as text. The so-called self-reflexive quality of modern literature is never an hermetic self-mirroring but an inevitable reworking of its own mimetic illusion, hence a maiming or distortion, a doubling and fraying of representation. If H.D. was, as Pound called her, the model "Imagiste," she was also one of those who quickly defined the limits of Imagism as a doctrinaire theory of style. Her own poetry reworked the notion of the Image, as surely as Pound reworked it in Vorticism and in the *Cantos*, in a way to indicate that a "presentation" which precedes "representation" (to recall Pound's terminology) is the grounding of poetry in its own textual complications—in the double movement of a text that tries at the same time to maintain the illusion of its fidelity to an external event or to nature and to falsify the event. The Image in this sense is an analytical scene.

Pound called the poetic Image (which included the "complex" of image, and hence the whole poem) "interpretative metaphor." And without any sense of contradiction, he overlayed the metaphor of the organic poem with the metaphor of the electrical circuit or system of transferences. (See, for exam-

[handwritten margin note: So image translates what we see but can hear]

ple, his own compilation in essay form of Ernest Fenellosa's notes on the Ideogram, "The Chinese Written Character as a Medium for Poetry.") The Image as translation (or better, as transcription and hence reinscription) could only effect a distortion, a script, producing a poem that could never be whole, could never totalize or remythologize the texts it appropriated. The coincidence between the interpretation and any uninterpreted event that might have preceded and given rise to it (the event whose textuality is forgotten) remains as problematic as it does in Nietzsche. The interpretation is inextricable from the tangle of the origin. Like the mystery of the Oedipal crossing, there is never any pure reality to be recuperated. Or to put it another way, the family romance could only have originated at a crossroads of two texts which never meet. It does not define Oedipus's genealogy, a repressed family line that might properly account for his birth, but inserts itself belatedly as the mark primordially disrupting or fraying that line. The family romance is both a complex and a question mark, that which precludes the unfolding of a sentence or the closing of a narrative. It is a poem that originarily opens poetry.

II

[handwritten margin note: poems in late Imagist style]

In the early 1930s, H.D. became an analysand of Freud, participating in two rather brief sessions, broken by a year's hiatus. Appropriately, the analysis was never finished, if indeed analysis can ever be said to close, though at the time its termination did not seem desired by either, but the result of historical circumstances. A decade later, during the most intense period of World War II, H.D. began to write poetry in what was to become known as her late, post-Imagist style, long poems of which the first and perhaps greatest is *The Walls Do Not Fall*, the first third of *Trilogy* (once called *War Trilogy*, and including as its second and third parts *Tribute to the Angels* and *The Flowering of the Rod*).[2] She also began a kind of memoir, later entitled *Tribute to Freud*, reflecting on the period of her analysis. The *Tribute* was not published until 1956, and then, in 1974, it was republished posthumously by Norman Holmes Pearson in a text that included not only "Writing on the Wall" (as it had once been called) but also "Advent," a diary-like series of notes which she called a "gloss" on the meditation (*Tribute*, viii). The two texts do not exactly duplicate one another, though there are common themes, but compose a sort of palimpsest of supplementary reflections. Far from being either a simple diary or an autobiographical recounting of notes of the analysis, "Advent" is as literary a text as "Writing on the Wall"—made up of intertextual overlays, the one extending the other in often unexpected ways, dispersing rather than unifying the crucial dreams (the reference dreams, as it were) that form the material for the two analysts.

Tribute to Freud, like the analysis it pursues, is a hieroglyph of the analytic scene, but no less the allegorization of that scene as a poetic space. That poetic space, therefore, has at least two authors, and two analysts, and dialogically projects itself as a "writing on the wall," a writing that is at the same time an overwriting or transformation of writing. "Advent" names a beginning that has already begun, not in an experience that is accessible through dream analysis, but in the reconstructive activity of analysis itself, including all its deformations. Little wonder, then, that H.D. recalls the analysis as a kind of restoration, of the "house" (and family), a rememorization of her earlier life that displaces the house with a "Cathedral." For the cathedral becomes her figure of the scene of analysis: "We are all haunted houses," she reflects in "Advent," and the "house in some indescribable way depends on the father-mother" (*Tribute*, 146). Yet, she has been dreaming of a cathedral, and it is the cathedral, not the house, that is "all important," because inside the "Cathedral we find regeneration or reintegration. This room [Freud's office] is the Cathedral": "The house is home, the house is the Cathedral. He wanted me to feel at home here" (*Tribute*, 146). Here the uncanny would not threaten.

The scene of reconstruction is a sanctuary within a space (a metaphor within a metaphor) like a crypt within a house, and Freud's study, filled with Etruscan and Egyptian artifacts, is like a cathedral reduplicating a mausoleum, a pyramid. The only space where reconstruction can take place, Freud's house/ ho-

cathedral consists of signs, memory objects, but also artifacts antedating all personal memory. H.D. recalls one of Freud's objects in particular, a "broken wood dog" (sign of Osiris?), a "toy from a tomb in Egypt," which reminds her of Freud's dog Yoti and his daughter Anna's Wulf. The analysis has also been a kind of rememorization, hence reentombment, since the reuniting of signs, the reconstruction of the family, not only suggests the father's death but the whole series of displacements uncovered by an analysis of the "family romance": "Yes (I repeated), the Cathedral of my dream was Sigmund Freud. 'No,' he said, 'not me—but analysis'" (*Tribute*, 146–47). Freud, the professor, the father-surrogate, is only another name of the father, as analytical origin.

His "house," therefore, which reduplicates her childhood house, is a scene of analysis, where the forces of reconstruction and distortion are simultaneously at play. For reconstruction (whether it suggests recuperation of a forgotten or repressed memory or a mimetic repetition of some earlier state) is not separable from deconstruction, since the process of reworking involves not only distortion but a re-marking of the distortion. The cathedral of analysis marks itself as a dream, and the dream is already an image-substitution and distortion in need of analysis. Like Freud's "uncanny" (*das Unheimlich*) the imaginary or poetic reconstruction of the house involves a distortion or change of context, a mixing of the homelike and unhomelike, a breaking of context. The analytical scene must, therefore, double or put into question the dream's navel and the house's father. If as Freud says, the cathedral is analysis, the father/professor/analyst is never its center but the sign of its centerlessness, of two forces at work.

At the very beginning of "Writing on the Wall," H.D. recapitulates the break in time, marked by Freud's death and the war, that lies between her analysis and the quest to recover what the analysis had unveiled, the "house" or "family." Yet, her text can only reconstruct the analysis which, far from restoring her family, had doubled her anxiety about her own participation in its disintegration. Freud, already the ambivalent substitute of her own father, a professor, marks the breach of time—Freud who had "brought the past into the present," who had broken the notion of time's depth, but by advocating a kind of elliptical repetition/distortion which forever deferred any thinking of analysis as making possible a repetition of the same. The war now doubly marks Freud's death as the death not only of the father but of the analyst, the ambivalence of analysis itself. It is another sign of the uncanny desire to restore the home, of a history that is, unlike Freud's in *Moses and Monotheism*, without a hero. The war is a "cataract." And H.D. recalls that when she was in analysis, analyst and analysand together had "touched lightly on some of the more abstruse transcendental problems . . . but we related them to the familiar family-complex" (*Tribute*, 13–14).

Now, in her dream of a "memory" she must recapitulate what is latent and even repressed of the pre-war (WWI) memory, the ambivalences of the "family-complex" itself. For in her reconstruction the deconstructive element of the "romance," itself both an allegory and an analytical instrument, becomes more evident, like her "bell-jar" dream or the palimpsest she recognizes to be the layered text of her life. As a writer, she interprets her memories by the use of mythological and literary parallels, but these texts are not unambiguous. Nor are her memories uncontaminated by the dreamwork, by being reworked in terms of a literate consciousness. Like the heroine of her late long poem *Helen in Egypt*, "*She herself is the writing*," but the "she" no longer has a place. She is always other, like a character in one of the images of her dream, a substitute for a substitute. Her dreams are already structured like a text.

Freud was at work on the early essays of *Moses and Monotheism* during the period of H.D.'s analysis, and she alludes to its significance in her *Tribute*:

it was in the desert that Moses raised the standard, the old T or Tau-cross of Thoth of the Egyptians. The Professor had been working on a continuation of his 'Moses, the Egyptian' theme, though we had not actually discussed this when I had my 'real' dream of the Egyptian princess. The professor asked me then if I were the child Miriam who in the Doré picture [the "illustrated Doré Bible" pictures entitled *Moses in the Bulrushes*] had stood, half-hidden in the river reeds, watching over the new-born child who was to become leader of a captive people and founder of a new religion, Miriam? Mignon? (108)

Earlier they had discussed the Egyptian theme and the Doré illustration as "hieroglyph" links in her "Princess" dream, the most clearly defined of all her dreams. She had, as she recalls, discussed with Freud "a few real dreams, some intermediate dreams that contained real imagery or whose 'hieroglyph' linked with authentic images and some quaint, trivial mocking dreams" (*Tribute*, 36). Though she can characterize dreams along a scale from "real" and "authentic" to "trivial" (in *The Walls Do Not Fall* she reflects that "gods have been smashed before // and idols and their secret is stored / in man's very speech, // in the trivial or / the real dream") (*Trilogy*, 151), a dream unveils nothing outside of a chain of associations with other dreams. Nor can it be interpreted without being re-worked in another dream, so that the authentic and real are already textual in origin. Thus Thoth's mark of the physician and of writing is appropriate to Freud and his Moses theme, though the cross of Thoth is identified by H.D. with her "serpent and thistle" dream (to which I return later), as a sign of writing the significance of which awaits later associations.

The Princess dream, therefore, is worked through both Freud's and the Biblical text, and more particularly through the illustrations of the Doré Bible, until it becomes a multi-layered Image of Miriam/Isis, of the princess who retrieves the child from the waters (or restores fragments into a figural whole, restores Osiris), thereby becoming the true "founder of a new religion" (*Tribute*, 36–37). As H.D. continues, "any dabbler with the theories of psychoanalysis" can read this dream in the frame of the "family-complex"; and she recalls her own anxieties when as a little girl she would bring her doll to her father's study, contesting with her more martially accoutred brother for the attention of the "*Father*, aloof, distant, the provider, the protector—but a little un-get-at-able, a little too far away and giant-like in proportion," unlike the "*Mother*" who signified "a virgin" (*Tribute*, 38). If one reads the language of ego-psychology (here, the Oedipal or castration dream as Freud would call it) in the language of mythology, and hence as the interpretation of interpretation, the "family triangle," as H.D. calls it, comes to signify not simply a child's anxiety but, as Freud himself hinted, a crisis of analysis. As Freud reads the recollection, the "doll" is the "symbol for the dream" itself, which projects a desire for the restoration of a family circle or triangle, a triangle that has been squared or opened. Hence the dream-wish of analysis, or poetic reconstruction, to restore some fragmented whole, underscores the question of a fragment and the desire for totalization. If one follows out this marking of the play in the analytic scene, where the analysis becomes a double scene of maintaining (or restoring) and reworking (maiming) the text, he or she may conclude that it doubles as a dream of poetry itself in H.D.'s mythology.

The doll may very well be a symbol of castration, as any dabbler in Freud must acknowledge, and hence the sign of a daughter's doubled restoration/displacement of the father/brother. A phallic symbol, then? the sign of a writer's maimed authority? of a tangled genealogy, whose doubled origin of father/mother the writer desires to recuperate? hence, the ambivalent movement of the stylus which restores and tears?

The phallus or stylus, here identified with the child's gift, is in Freud's sense the uncanny sign of a castration in which writing is always implicated, if writing is thought of in the classical sense of a proper representation or substitute for presence and a restoration of meaning. The doll as "symbol of the dream" is a poem/gift, and the poem is analytical, not expressive. To read H.D. here, recounting her and Freud's mutual analysis of the princess dream, is not to confront a crisis in H.D.'s early life so much as to confront the crisis of writing and hence of representation and authority, the problematic identity of the author. Castration fear, as poststructural interpreters of Freud make evident, is never neurosis manifest in the simple perception of an absence, but a complication of perception itself which indelibly poses a question of absence and what represents it. The dream of the princess who restores Moses, of the daughter who gives birth to the male child, the "founder of a new religion," is the dream of recuperating the family complex as a scene of interpretation, where the father's role is unambiguous. But the restoration can never be complete, nor simple, since analysis always uncovers the complex or tangle of the origin, and hence of the father's role. The "house" turns out to be the cathedral, and the father already represented by an intermediary, the physician who is both poet and analyst. Moreover, the "founder of a new religion," like Moses, has had to be born again, saved, as it were, by translation. And H.D. is quick to note that Freud called his disciple and translator, Marie Bonaparte, the "Princess," the "obvious mother-symbol" (*Tribute*, 39).

Analysis as restoration involves a double movement of castration (which can never be perceived, just as the woman signified a phallus that is never seen and therefore never properly represented, even by a surrogate). Hence castration involves at once a maiming and a restoration of sorts, since it is the sign of both the father and the son, of the tangle of father and son, as much as it is a sign of women. Throughout H.D.'s text, Freud speculates on the poet's compulsion to identify: (1) with her mother, (2) with her father, (3) with her brother, and (4) with surrogates for each, one of which, the text makes clear, is Freud himself. Freud the professor now stands ambivalently for her own father/professor, a mathematician and astronomer, seeker of origins whose signs were his office sanctuary and his library. Her father is identified with a "study . . . lined with books," a room otherwise decorated with but one picture and adorned with a "white owl under a bell-jar" and a human skull (*Tribute*, 19–34). She remembers him writing "rows on rows of numbers, but I could then scarcely distinguish the shape of a number from a letter" (*Tribute*, 19). H.D. thinks of this hermetic, tomb-like space, as a deathly scene, an enclosure of scientific self-reflexivity. Just as his triangular or pyramidal paperweight reflects repetitiously the room as a closed cosmos, the father derives his authority from a kind of interpretation based on the ideal of representation, the book of the cosmos. It is a strangely narcissistic study, in contrast to Freud's, which has fewer volumes and is dominated by his own writing and the signs of its dissemination through the work of disciples, interpreters, translators: "compilations of his followers, disciples, and pseudo-disciples and imitators," which open the room's three-dimensional gathering of past, present, and future into "another time-element," the "fourth-dimensional" (*Tribute*, 23). Freud's study, indeed, textualized the professor, who is signified not only by his library and the interpretations which project far beyond its scientific formulations, but by his Etruscan and Egyptian artifacts, unquestionable phallic signs, signifiers whose indeterminacy sets off a proliferation of meanings. As Michel Foucault has said of Freud's canon, this study/text produces interpretations that can never be determined by the text, as readings of Freud lead to discourses quite different from psychoanalysis. Freud's study, then, is the cathedral of analysis which, like that of the oracle of Delphi, demands translation or interpretation, demands disciples, projects itself through a stylus which is held in no one hand. In a canceled passage of the holograph of "Writing on the Wall" (now in the Beinecke collection), she writes, "Was it 'by chance or intention' that he linked me in his creative, vivid discrimination with translation, with art, with this accredited greatest of living renaissance innovators, thinkers, and artists [da Vinci]?"

Tribute to Freud emphatically stresses H.D.'s identification with her mother above all others. Even her sibling rivalry with her brother (who did in fact succeed his father as Director of the Flower Astronomical Observatory near Philadelphia) takes a simple competitive form, to be the first in her father's "eye" (for which the Freudian sign of castration might be evoked). But this competition is superseded by a need to preempt the brother's claim upon her mother, the father's second wife, to succeed in the role of she who restores or maintains, as if by translation. But one must caution against reading this as the working out of a personal neurosis, particularly since *Tribute* is written in the wake of an analysis that has begun by making it clear that the family complex is the interpretative frame both analyst and analysand will use, a metaphor for metaphysical themes. The mother, a second wife, marks the family tangle more distinctly than does any antagonistic relation of father and son. Just as the princess of the dream restores Moses the child, restores him not as the representative or simple origin, but as a textual complication, the dream repeats the very question of origins Freud has posed in *Moses and Monotheism*, arguing that Moses was an Egyptian and that the Moses who speaks through the prophetic texts of the Judeo-Christian tradition was at least two accidentally compounded historical figures. The mother with whom H.D. identifies, whom she seeks in her restoration of the past, becomes the ambivalent figure of the poet as both translator and translation, the translator who is at once the conserver of the text and its surrogate author. The dream, as we will see, is a question mark, the very mark of writing.

Tribute to Freud, then, allegorizes a kind of murder (which includes the maiming of writing) in that it recounts the displacement and restoration of the father in the family complex, but not as any simple substitute of Professor Freud for Professor Doolittle. On the contrary, what is undone and reworked is the allegory of writing itself. If her father's study represents the fiction of representation, H.D.'s description exposes its hermetic blindness—a library centered upon a paperweight which is nothing but an empty reflecting surface. The pyramidal, representational machine at the center is as empty as Hegel's pyramid, concealing only a sign of absence. But the Freudian scene deconstructs the same family complex that it appropriates as an analytical instrument, making representation unthinkable without repression. What H.D. brings to Freud's room is the already doubled figure of the woman/translator/poet—hence the woman as the body of the text, neither presence nor absence, but the sign of the sign. Helen (and this was her mother's name, like that of the goddess) "*is the writing*" in the sense that she is the fecundity, the multiplicity or heterogeneity, of the text; neither presence nor absence, she not only represents but disseminates. And as Derrida remarks of Nietzsche's women, she is not "style" but "styles," and related to castration only in the sense that nothing can be known about her; not style as the unveiling of truth or meaning, nor even style as veiling or concealing: "the insinuation of the woman (of) Nietzsche is that, if there is going to be style, there can only be more than one," a fracturing, disseminating writing that precludes any thought of restoration or recuperation: "There is no such thing as a woman, as truth in itself of woman in itself."[3] Translation, poetry, castration—the woman is translation (*the writing*) not because she is without a penis but because she signifies the duplicitous sense of the phallus, which has no place, cannot be reduced to meaning. It is a sign that radicalizes the thinking of "truth" and its recuperation: "Indeed, there is no such thing as truth in itself. But only surfeit of it. Even if it should be for me, about me, truth is plural" (*Spurs*, 81).

It is the woman, then, who saves or gives birth (a second or belated birth) to the "founder of a new religion," by the force of her heterogeneity, her ambivalent role that obscures not only the origin of the child (like Freud's Moses) but provides it with a genealogical fiction. The woman is a text for H.D. as she is for both Freud and Nietzsche—not a proper displacement or representation but a spurring, signifying force. Just as Freud is a Moses for H.D., the new religion of analysis (emblematized by the cathedral) is sustained only by a textuality that both dissimulates hiding a mystery and distorts or wrenches the simulacrum, so as to open interpretation. All the women in Freud's life—Anna, Marie Bonaparte, H.D. herself—become for H.D. the fecund multiplicity of his utterance, the virulence and the cure of writing. The woman, then, is the doubled center of the Freudian scene, the sign of the always displaced center of the Freudian scene of analysis. She is not an alternative to the father, but uncanny, the sign of a translation that does not reproduce presence or meaning but disperses meanings, like a text. The tainted (and for some chauvinist) vocabulary, which we have borrowed directly from H.D. and from Freud, can never itself have any direct reference to sexual politics. For, H.D.'s poetics, like her dream, appropriates Freud's family romance or family complex and restores those metaphors that have gone awry, which no longer promise the closure of analysis and the restoration of the "house," but that open a reading. And for H.D., the poem is a reading, and hence a scene of analysis, an uncanny yet homelike place of a double movement, the equivocal play of restoration and distortion displayed by the intertextuality of every text. A home away from home.

III

Over the last two decades of her life, H.D. was heavily committed to what might be called her autobiographical project. If her meditations on analysis turn out to be an analysis of her analysis, which renewed her poetic energies, and *Trilogy* is the poetic complement of "Writing on the Wall," *Tribute* is also an anomalous chapter in a sequence of narratives (many of which remain in unpublished manuscripts in the Beinecke Library collection) that attempt a reconstruction of her own ancestry. *Bid Me To Live*, her more or less official, if barely fictionalized, autobiography, is one of the few published chapters of an extended and incomplete family romance. One of the manuscripts, *End of Torment*, is an elegiac reminiscence on the odyssey of Pound's late life, and a testimony of her enduring love: "To recall Ezra," she writes, is "to recall my father"; "To recall my father is to recall the cold, blazing intelligence of my 'last attachment' of the war-years in London." Other texts, projected or completed, were to form a series collectively entitled *The Gift*. Notes on this series, to which *Bid Me To Live* (once called *Madrigal*) and *End of Torment* are supplementary, suggest that *Tribute to Freud* is a kind of discourse on her method of restoration. The texts of *The Gift* are made possible by analysis, reconstructions of the Doolittle family history in what she calls the form of a "Greek novel," one chapter of which was to be called *White Rose and Red*, a fictional reminiscence on the Pre-Raphaelite Brotherhood. (If this manuscript is extant I have not seen it.) H.D.'s only connection with the Rossetti circle was, as she notes, the kind of arbitrary association uncovered by analysis, and literally by writing, the uncovering of a kind of repetition made possible by the discovery in one life of a single element or sign from the other. Each reconstruction of her life (whether her own, or that of her parents or grandparents) is composed out of a "child's alphabet chart," which guarantees that her contemporary life has been some kind of repetition of the earlier. A daughter of Helen, born in Bethlehem, she is, like Helen of *Helen in Egypt*, "*the writing*." What she calls her "psychical communication" with the Rossetti circle, then, reaches back also to the Dante circle, and is translated into a contemporary link through the William Morris tripod table on which she writes. Norman Pearson had remarked in his introduction to *The Gift* on William Morris as a "spiritual father" (xii), and H.D. sometimes fantasized herself as an Elizabeth Siddal, receiving messages through the Morris table, itself already a surviving sign of the oracle of Delphi whose tripod put her in contact with the "ABC" of writing.

The tripod, as one might expect, is excavated once more in the *Tribute*, a "shadow" at the uncertain center of the central dream or hieroglyph that gives its name to the text itself, "Writing on the Wall." There, in the picture on the wall which H.D. fancied she saw as a dream while writing in a room on the island of Corfu in 1920, and which she recounted to Freud as the primary symptom for analysis, the central image is the "shadow"—not a shadow on light but a shadow on which a dim light showed, the silhouette, she queries, of a "dead brother? lost friend?" Freud translated her dream as a "desire for union with [her] mother" (*Tribute*, p. 44), but only after she translated the silhouette into a "design," a "neat trick, a shortcut, a pun, a sort of joke": "For the three-legged lamp-stand in the miscellaneous clutter on the wash-stand is none other than our old friend, the tripod of the classic Delphi . . . this venerable object of the cult of the sun god, symbol of poetry and prophecy" (*Tribute*, 46). The tripod symptom is at once the most venerable and most common, yet abnormal, of symbols, the sign of the sign itself, a "hieroglyph" that demands reading: both translation and interpretation. For what the oracle reveals (always indirectly) at Delphi is never simple. As H.D. recalls, the Delphic utterance is always rendered through the "Pythoness" who attends the sacred place. What is revealed at Delphi is, like a "writing on the wall," made up of signs of overlayed texts.

H.D. seems to acknowledge the ninety-third fragment of Heraclitus: "The lord [or master] whose oracle is at Delphi: he does not speak, he does not conceal, he makes [or gives] signs." Modern critical scholarship has begun to extricate the problematic of this fragment from the metaphysical readings that have suppressed the question of the sign, that read the oracle's sign as *aletheia*. For the problematic of the oracle, as Clemence Ramnoux has argued, lies precisely in the impossibility of clarifying the oracle's utterance without posing another question: the *si*, of deciding that it means this *if* or that *if*—hence of dividing the utterance, of deciding whether the sign might mean this or that under certain conditions (*if*) when the sign is *unde-*

cidable. This problematic also takes the form of hypothesizing a privileged reader or interpreter, one who believes or has faith that the word can never deceive, thus posing the further question of the obscurity of the sign versus against the clarity of speech, therefore underwriting the "*double sens*" of every oracular signature. The oracle does not reveal (or speak), nor does it deceive (or conceal), but in making signs it discourses; or as Ramnoux reads it: "The signs of the world and my discourse conceal and say exactly the same thing," say by concealing, conceal by saying.[4] To put one's trust in a translator or this "double sense" is to see the translation as privileged, as a language that renders the concealed, a common privilege accorded the poet and poetry. But the poet as translator, the woman as translation, does not reveal; she discourses in the double sense of the image or sign. The discourse (or translation) divides the utterance not only from any origin but from itself; the sign of the oracle was originally free floating or disseminated, that is, translated, textualized as a writing of an unheard voice.

The understanding of H.D.'s poetics—and in a sense the thrust of poetic modernism—must be situated in this problematic of the oracular sign and in the question of style (or styles), of the hieroglyph, of dream-writing. Like the metaphysical readings of Heraclitus, which give us a decidable either/or reading yet acknowledge that the oracle's wisdom exceeds the limits of human understanding, H.D.'s poetics has been interpreted in terms of prophecy or mystical revelations, as an archeological uncovering of the secrets concealed in ancient words or texts. Norman Pearson writes in his introduction to the posthumously published *Hermetic Definition,* "Like many Freudians, she became quasi-Jungian and could bring the cabala, astrology, magic, Christianity, classical and Egyptian mythology, and personal experience into a joint sense of Ancient Wisdom" (vi). The cabala, however, and we have only to witness Harold Bloom's appropriation of it, is not necessarily a mystical text of revelations or even a dream book, but only a machine for interpretation, and hence for misprision. H.D.'s alleged Jungianism, and mysticism, is the issue of a blind or idealized reading of her texts that ignores her own problematizing of the image, her

own deployment of the text as an analytic. The play between deconstruction and reconstruction, in both her poems and her
prose, characterizes (literally and figuratively) this problematic.
If for her a poem affirms by *feeling* "the meaning that words
hide," that words are "anagrams, cryptograms, / little boxes,
conditioned // to hatch butterflies," their revelation is never
direct or simple; the poem always remains "jottings on a margin, / indecipherable palimpsest scribbled over // with too
many contradictory emotions" (*Trilogy*, 53, 42). The image is
never congruent with its origin, its origin never evident outside
of the images doubling or distorting, and hence dispersing it.
The unconscious is not a reservoir of some untapped truth, but
a chaos:

> Depth of the sub-conscious spews forth
> too many incongruent monsters
>
> and fixed indigestible matter
> such as shell, pearl; imagery
>
> done to death; perilous ascent,
> ridiculous descent; rhyme, jingle,
>
> overworked assonance, nonsense,
> juxtaposition of words for words' sake,
>
> without meaning, undefined . . .
> (*Trilogy*, 44)

The poem originates in a place (or a scene) of extraordinary
heterogeneity, and proceeds not by opening or unconcealing,
but by layering. Yet, it can never reconstruct an original model,
let alone a simple origin, or recuperate some original whole,
since any notion of the origin (as represented, say, in the "family-complex" by the home) is already only one of the images.
Reconstruction involves reading/writing, translation, and distortion. Every poem reveals its own operation, or describes its
own sense, therefore, because it conceals by revealing, reveals
by concealing. A passage in *The Flowering of the Rod* says it with
concise ambivalence:

And no one will ever know
whether the picture he saw clearly

as in a mirror was pre-determined
by his discipline and study

of old lore and by his innate capacity
for transcribing and translating

the difficult secret symbols
       . . . .
no one will ever know
whether it was a sort of spiritual optical illusion,
or whether he looked down the deep deep-well

of the so-far unknown
depths of pre-history . . .

(Trilogy, 165)

She is probably allegorizing Freud and/or Pound here, as
the Magus to whom she is a Mary, but the allusion is of little
matter. In the *Tribute*, the central dreams—the princess dreams
and the "Writing on the Wall"—signify the same question, since
they have no bottom, no origin in a single event, but originate
in what is already a hieroglyph or maimed text. They begin, as
at Delphi or at the writing desk, in a double reading/writing of
the sign:

> *Signet*—as from sign, a mark, token, proof; signet—the privy seal, a
> seal; signet-ring—a ring with a signet or private seal; sign-manuel—the
> royal signature, usually a mention of the sovereign's name. (I have
> used my initials H.D. consistently as my writing signet or sign-manuel,
> though it is only, at this moment, as I checked up on the word 'signet'
> in my Chambers' English Dictionary that I realized that my writing sig-
> nature has anything remotely suggesting sovereignty or the royal man-
> ner.) Sign again—a word, gesture, symbol, or mark, intended to signify
> something else. Sign again—(medical) a symptom, (astronomical)
> one of the twelve parts of the Zodiac. (*Tribute*, 66)

H.D.'s "writing on the wall" dream is never interpreted, except as a question of the sign, which must always be read in "two
ways or in more than two ways": either as the "suppressed desire
for 'signs and wonders'" and hence as the "suppressed desire to
be a Prophetess"; or as mere illustration or representations, im-

ages borrowed from an actual dream to *"echo"* an idea (*Tribute,* 51). Yet this last is not simple representation or expression but something like a dreamwork which reworks a repression, thus protecting against a "freak" idea or "dangerous symptom." Poetry need not be identified with neurosis, but it is never immediate, and always a distortion or reworking of other images. Poetry, like Freud's "complex," is Mosaic. One may desire to read it as containing one symbol that determines all the others, like the "sun" of H.D.'s hieroglyphic "Writing on the Wall," but no sign can be extricated as central or singular. It can only be "read," and this reading always involves another, just as does any scene of analysis (*Tribute,* 56).

It is significant, then, that the "writing on the wall" dream or daydream is read in conjunction with an even earlier, childhood dream, which H.D. calls her "serpent and thistle" dream—a vision or picture of an "alter-shaped block of stone," divided in two by a rough curved line, a stone cut mark: "In one half or section, there was a serpent, roughly carved; it was conventionally coiled with head erect; on the other side, there was a roughly incised, naturalistic yet conventionally drawn thistle" (*Tribute,* 64). Ezra Pound had helped her interpret this dream, with the assistance of reference books and concordances from his parents' library, which he used much as one would employ a dream book. Pound called it a "flashback in time or a prevision of some future" that concerned Asklepois, child of Apollo, patron of healers, whose sign, the serpent, is a symbol of both death and resurrection. But Pound could not account for the thistle, except as an ornament, and H.D. was never able to recall seeing the two in combination other than in her dream; except for one instance, a small Hellenistic signet-ring she discovered one day in 1911 at the Louvre. The thistle comes to remind her of a spear, a sign she interprets years later to signify an absence, like the figure of Wingless Victory or Nike A-pteros that Freud shows her: "'She is perfect,' he said, '*only she has lost her spear*'" (*Tribute,* 69).

Now the two dreams, two hieroglyphs, fold over one another. Another of Freud's objects, an ivory Indian figure of a seated Vishnu surrounded and covered by a dome of serpents, recalls the Corfu dream, the "writing on the wall," the most enigmatic

and abstract signs of the writing: "a half-S, which might have re-
called the scroll pattern of the inverted *S* or incomplete question mark in the picture series on the wall" (*Tribute*, 67). H.D.
does eventually translate or interpret these signs, but not with
the help of Pound's dream book. Rather, she interprets more
in the spirit of Freud's rebus, the dream as code instead of the
dream as symbol. But the reading turns out to be a radical reworking, an uncovering of what she calls the "common prop-
erty of the whole," the "universal language" of the dream which
man spoke "as at the beginning of time" (*Tribute*, 71). What she
deciphers as a hieroglyph is reworked as a hieroglyph, a single
word that is originally heterogeneous. That word is any one of
the names for Freud himself—professor, cathedral, Sigmund:

> My serpent-and-thistle motive, for instance, or *Leitmotif*, I had almost
> written. It was a sign, a symbol certainly. . . . My serpent and thistle—
> what did it remind me of? There was Aaron's rod, of course, which
> when flung into the ground turned into a living reptile. Reptile?
> Aaron's rod, if I am not mistaken, was originally the staff of Moses.
> There was Moses in the bulrushes, "our" dream and "our" Princess.
> There was the ground, cursed by God because Adam and Eve had
> eaten the Fruit of the Tree. Henceforth, it would bring forth thorns
> and thistles—thorns, thistles, the words conjure up the same scene,
> the barren, unproductive waste or desert. *Do men gather grapes of thorns,
> or figs of thistles?* Another question, another question mark, a half-S,
> the other way round, *S* for seal, symbol, serpent certainly, signet, Sig-
> mund.
>   *Sigmund*, the singing voice; no, it is Siegmund really, the victorious
> mouth or voice or utterance. There was Victory, our sign on the wall,
> our hieroglyph, our writing. (*Tribute*, 87–88)

"Our writing" represents a question of signs, signs as (questions) marks. Like the recollection of Bergasse (Freud's street,
a hill and a path, a design, she writes, crowned by *acanthus*, the
prickly plant, the thistle). It was H.D., we recall, who alone had
been able to remember serpent and thistle ("Thy rod and thy
staff"), emblems of the most radical incongruence, yet emblems of Freud and herself, of analyst and poet, in a dream that
antedated her analysis by decades. But this singular combination will not yield to a Freudian reading, to the symbol serpent
or the symbol thistle, the spear and the spearless, male and fe-

male. H.D. has momentarily excavated a site, only to discover that what is at its center is uncanny, an undoing of the emblem of the family as some archetypal and original moment. For the serpent is language, language as the mark, the sign, the question. And the thistle is the double sign of the phallus, of the undecidable, the mark of a writing as a castration that never occurred. Neither presence or absence nor the sign presence or absence, it is the signifier of the signifier—the stylus, both the mark and the origin of the mark, the sign of writing as dissemination.

"Our hieroglyph"—"Put H.D. in the place of Sigmund Freud" (*Tribute*, 74), she had proposed, imagining the possibility of turning upside down the "hourglass" of vulgar time, of the poet displacing the analyst who had proclaimed the poet's first-ness. The translator speaks by translation, in an *Alcestis*-like economy of writing, in the theft that is writing. "*Stop thief,*" she exclaims, in yet another leitmotif of the *Tribute*. Thoth and Hermes, those names of writing, are no less names of Freud. But Isis is also the name of the writer, the rememberer. Only the poet has style, is both the writer and the writing, serpent and thistle, the irreducible double. Only the poet remembers this curious combination, as an uncanny double inscription on a rock, the double mark of which the only name is *signet*. An uncanny marriage: "There are dreams or sequences of dreams that follow a line like a graph or a map or show a jagged triangular pattern, like a crack on a bowl that shows the bowl or vase may at any moment fall to pieces" (*Tribute*, 93). Similarly a poem, which reflects its own operations; it cannot mirror its own whole-ness, but only its distortive reworking. It is not sincere (sin-cere, that is, without the wax that might cover over the flaw or the crack), but a golden bowl, like Henry James's, that is always already flawed. H.D.'s signature repeats the sign of the poet, the serpent of the text, its question, doubly marked by a thistle or stylus which both writes and is written, is and is not, like a phallus. Let her (who is the "*writing*") have the last words: "She asks the question. Each verse of the lyric is a question or a series of questions. Do you know the Land? Do you know the House? Do you know the Mountain? / *Kennst du den Berg und seinen Wolkensteg?* / 'Do you know the mountain and its cloud-bridge?'" This is an awkward enough translation but the idea of mountain and bridge is so very suitable to this whole *translation* of the Professor and our work together. *Steg* really means a plank; *foot-bridge* is the more accurate rendering. It is not a bridge for a great crowd of people, and it is a bridge flung, as it were, across the abyss, not built and hammered and constructed. There is plenty of psychoanalytic building and constructing: "We are dealing with the realm of fantasy and imagination, flung across the abyss, and these are the poet's lines" (*Tribute*, 108).

POSTSCRIPT: IN OTHER WORDS

There is a certain inevitability to the Postscript, since it marks not some aftering but only the limit of any first or last word. Did H.D. have the last word, even in the passage I quoted, a translation and a discourse on translation? A carrying over and an attempt to bridge over the artifices of such a bridge? H.D. lingers upon the question of the bridge and the abyss. Which is artifice? What produces the need of the other? Does the bridge overcome the abyss or mark it? Is not the bridge the form of the abyss?

The editor requests that I provide a context for my reading of H.D.'s text.[5] A theory perhaps, since my essay is a reading of a text and not the extrapolation from it of a theoretical statement or a set of theoretical assertions. Indeed, he seems to ask, why this resistance to theory in an essay commissioned for a collection on theory? Why this rendering of H.D.'s text as at once theoretical and atheoretical? Is H.D. a theorist of modernism or a tributary of Freud? What is in question here is precisely the status of her text, and in turn of poetry. A question of translation, as she aptly puts it. And as a question of translation, a problematic that is inscribed at the epicenters of contemporary criticism.

After all, H.D. offers us more than a pretext that she is remembering an analysand's experience, even if the reconstruction has to take the form of a certain fictionalized transference, and even if the documentary form includes two texts or two versions. Is the text, then, autobiographical? a remembrance or a reading of Freud? an analysis (hers? theirs?) of her dreams? or a narrative of analysis? of dreams as analysis? Or is it, perhaps, a kind of quest romance, a poetic reflection upon the myths of poetic creation?

Interpretation and translation obviously play crucial roles in this reflection, particularly since the search for origins poses at its very beginning a question of analysis and of method. There are questions, perhaps, which perpetuate speculation by precluding its closure or resolution, and thus fracture the dream of speculation or self-referentiality: of a text which could be at the same time methodical and a discourse on its method, or a poem which could be at the same time a representation and a meta-commentary on poetics. I placed a great deal of emphasis on the moment in "Writing on the Wall" when H.D. announced that she and Freud would employ the metaphor of the family complex to reflect on metaphysical issues. Among those issues is the status of the metaphor itself, the family complex or family romance being already derived from literature or myth to stand as an emblem for some law of origins, a genealogy of history as well as of a psychic life. For Freud, then, the family romance is not only a figure which represents the order of history, the regulation of succession and restoration; it is a figure in the employ of the analyst. Both a figure for analysis and an analysis.

The metaphor of the family romance inscribes, in a multiple of sense, its own doubleness. Derived from myth for use as an analytical model, the figure is reinscribed into literature by criticism either as a structural paradigm (e.g., for revealing the genealogical structure of narrative) or as a regulative trope (e.g., Harold Bloom's theory of influence and intertextuality). It becomes both the theme and form of a certain temporal mode that theorists now want to set in opposition to the privileged spatial form of lyric. But it is not simply a figure of opposition or antithesis, of history as opposed to universality, since it bears within itself an irreducible difference (or even *différance*): it is a figure of figure, of the chiasmus or crossing, a figure which erases and marks a problem of representation (and of naming) even as it promises some kind of orderly if deferred restoration, some kind of corrected genealogy. The prefigured story of the Oedipal crossroads, then, inscribes the doubleness of literature: the dream of a corrected line, a restored genealogy, and a clarified perception, even as it introduces the critical riddle or fate of interpretation. The metaphor, thus, indexes literature and criticism in a way that suggests not only literature's inevitable impurity (or ultimate failure to achieve self-reflexiveness) but indicates its hermeneutic "stairway of surprise" (Emerson).

H.D. came to Freud, then, not simply as a poet to her analyst, to endure the satisfactions of some strange adoption, but as one aware of the original and originary critical (or is it diacritical?) nature of poetry. Whenever Freud indulges in the cliches of Freudianism, suggesting for example that she wanted "to be a boy" and a hero like Moses (*Tribute*, 120) and therefore not only wanted to displace her brother so as to be the son who would displace the father but wanted to identify with her companion Bryher (who in Freud's terms is "*only* a boy," though H.D. envisioned her in association with the "Pythoness of Delphi," the detached translator of Images, as we have seen)— whenever Freud reduces his own hermeneutical detachment into a protective repetition of his theory (becoming increasingly literal or allegorical), H.D. reintroduces the fact that they have been at work upon a hieroglyph, whether "Our hieroglyph" or a "hieroglyph of the unconscious" (*Tribute*, 88, 93). The thrust of this analysis, this search for poetic origins, is not, however, simply a resistance to the patriarch of analysis, of a matriarchal art to a patriarchal science (no more than it is, as some would want to read it, an argument like Graves's in support of a matriarchal tradition in poetry which supersedes the patriarchal western tradition). When H.D. reflects that Freud's probings tunnel deep but uncover only a "scene or picture from those [deep] realms" and that this "clearest fountain-head of highest truth" is irreducibly an "*illuminated manuscript*, and has its place in that category among books and manuscripts" where "books and the people merge in this world of fantasy and imagination," she reinscribes the origin into the false depth of a palimpsest, or better, a library. Her poet is therefore neither a sexual nor an asexual figure, but a figure, like the "Pythoness of Delphi," or perhaps, like Isis (the restorer) and Thoth (the physician, translator, thief). And the origin is a text, not in the material or colloquial sense of that word, but in the sense of an irreducibly figural or doubled being, of an origin that is always already displaced, of a poetic truth that begins in repetition (re-petition).

Freud's calling H.D. "translation" (in the cancelled passage, alas) is not gratuitous, then, although she manages at once to erase the designation and to turn it against his authoritarian, or fatherly, implication. In the first place, translation involves at least a double operation: a remembering of the dismembered and dispersed (Isis), and a theft that signifies an incorrigible displacement (Thoth). It at once rehearses the primary sense of a fall, loss, dispersal of some original language, and exposes the possibility that such an historical figure, both promising and prefiguring a future restoration, is as Nietzsche argued, the very work of language itself and not some truth it represents or expresses. The legend of Moses' stutter includes, albeit eccentrically, the death of the father, even as Nietzsche indicated that getting rid of God would necessitate the getting rid of grammar, or grammatology. Moses' stutter is already a figure for translation as criticism. And what is translation?

"What is translation?" Derrida asks in his long footnote to "Living On," an essay ostensibly of literary criticism.[6] The footnote also bears a title, "Border Lines," a translation of "Journal de Bord," an untranslatable phrase that includes the double sense of "shipboard journal" and "journal on *bord*," the latter sense being further untranslatable in that *bord* may imply either edge or ship, either margin or voyage, the double sense of an absolute demarcation and a space which regulates the legal crossing of boundaries or frontiers. The entire situation of this footnote that should ground the text but sets it afloat, erasing edges or contaminating those marginal demarcations that allow us to order the hierarchy of texts, of this meditation on translation that is to instruct a translator on the economy and limits of translation, reveals that it is a diversion that names the irreducible diversion of all notes. Or should one say the *foot*note is Oedipal? There are many questions which Derrida's note poses, and one is the pose of the note, its posture as ground and margin, particularly since its message to the translator includes the double bind that he must translate his instructions on translation, and *after*, one assumes, he has translated the *primary* text. The note has problematized every primary term, and left as primary the already freighted and derived notion of translation.

Readers of Derrida, not to say of the poets, of H.D., then, should be wary of what this privileging of "translation" instigates. First, there are his seemingly direct or cognitive statements, such as the remark that there are always two notions of translation, the normative one that suggests an orderly transfer of meaning, or signifieds, through an efficient displacement of signifiers, and the disseminative function which implies a radical displacement and a fracturing of meaning. Derrida, in short, must attack the question poetically, in an essay on poets who have above all else poetically insisted on the primacy of the question. And the question of translation, of "living on" or even carrying on and over, of continuity and genealogy, is a question of death, of that border where the system of orderly displacement must take place, that margin that Derrida often calls "text," itself already a figure and hence a translation and a breaking of what the metaphysicians call "Being" or "presence." A text includes death, includes translation, just as it includes a ciphered and deceptive account of its own origin; just as a text, always already derived (de:rived) is never its material or scriptive form, never that simple translation which some call representation and others expression.

When Derrida says, then, that "One never writes either in one's own language or in a foreign language," he reiterates the reiterative economy of translation: "This is my starting point: no meaning can be determined out of context, but no context permits saturation. . . . When a text quotes and requotes, with or without quotation marks, when it is written on the brink, you start, or indeed have already started, to lose your footing" (*Deconstruction and Criticism*, 101, 81–82). Derrida's riving of contexts, his "conning" of them, his de-control of reading, has become a sort of scandal for the Anglo-American metaphysics of taboo. But not for the poets who, Freud after all had said, were there before us. There? Where? At the translative beginning of (the fiction of) the origin. At (or about) the text. If poetry is the economy of dream, of what is dream the economy? Of poetry, H.D. and other poets seem to say; that is, dream is originarily poetic and critique.

It is not the nature of a truth that is translated or conveyed across some limit that H.D. thinks of when she thinks of poetry, on the model of psychoanalysis, as tapping the "springs" of a "deep" and accumulated "human consciousness." That "consciousness" of Freud's can only be prefigured as irreducibly metaphorical or diacritical, or as a "spring" of images (appearing in at least two languages) sealed up or blocked, so that to tap the spring one had to clear the blockage. But clearing the blockage does not simply release a present or immediate language. It involves a translation, writing, and reading. There is an "economy" involved, and H.D. underscores the pertinence of this metaphor (*Tribute*, 82–83). The analysand (or patient) is responsible for digging up the suppressed material, itself already figural, and the analyst is responsible for the "system" or economy of translation which can read the "*hieroglyph of the unconscious*" (*Tribute*, 93). Consciousness is irreducibly textual, and more precisely, intertextual, not only in the sense of a tropological relation between earlier and later texts (or in analysis, between the marks of some early primal trauma and its later and repeated occurrence or re-mark), but in the sense that every text is made up of a heterogeneity of textual elements and hence a con-text that cannot be saturated. Poetry, then, translates by breaking contexts.

At the point in "Writing on the Wall," where H.D. turns to the Goethe poem and hence to the question of translation I quoted at the end of the essay, her sense of poetry as an originally doubled notion of recuperation/translation becomes an unresolvable contradiction that only poetry itself can bridge over. Goethe's poem, beginning "Kennst du das Land" signifies the mother language of his consciousness (or unconscious), a metaphorical "Haus" made up, like Freud's study, of the artifacts of all human culture. But if Freud is at home here in (if his home is) this archeological site, where the repressed has been returned, H.D. has come from another land and has "brought nothing with me." Freud's study, like Goethe's poem, signifies "the tradition of an unbroken family" (*Tribute*, 97), and seems to promise a continuity or succession, but H.D.'s is the mother tongue of Poe who can only speak of the emptying out of the "Holy Land" of the "Psyche," and of some problematic and deferred unity, some crypt to be opened. When Freud's judgment is more rooted in the encumbered past, H.D.'s "Intuition" is swifter, she claims, and "challenges the Professor, though not in words" (*Tribute*, 99). This contest of "question and answer" as a play between analysis and poetry (between philosophy and poetry, as it were) is dramatized as a play between German and American, old and new world thought, a play which prefigures all beginnings in the Janus-like opposition of a translation that carries over and a translation that displaces and defers. Just as Goethe's poem raises problems for his translator, it raises questions about translation, about the continuity of a journey from a known "Land" to an unknown. Thus, H.D. notes, the poem is poised upon the abyss between question and answer, or poised upon its own curious signs which H.D. thinks of as "question marks" or reversed "S's," those serpents of language which mark its double nature, which signify that it is not simply a bridge between two worlds, a bridge over the abyss, but the sign of the abyss as well. It is in this abyss, this land of the psyche that is language, that H.D. locates the origins (or better, beginnings that displace origins) of poetry, the translated/translating thing itself, like the "Penelope's web" she is weaving (an instrument as well for unweaving). Poetry, then, is at once a re-weaving of earlier poems (an anthology of myths and texts) and an unweaving, a deferral, like Penelope's, that seems to make way for the return of the father yet marks the edifice of his restitution. Like Penelope in Stevens's "The World as Meditation," poetry seems to signify a return, a restoration, but what returns is uncertain, like a figure (a sun?) coming "constantly so near," but never fully arriving, like a figure that is remembered because it is "never forgotten." The "never forgotten" signifies the status of the "remembered," of the "re" which precedes its members (*Collected Poems*, 518–19).

The figur-ology of *Tribute to Freud,* which would authorize yet bridge over the displacement of the father, which would substitute the child for the father, but also for the mother, which implicates sexuality in textuality, folds into the double figure of the dream-text the question of death and translation, of the substitutive mechanism itself. It is a figuration, as it were, of the poem as body-image and as figural ground, doubly bound to the task of signifying the moment; as H.D. puts it, "an exact moment," when "the boat slipped into enchantment" or when "'crossing the line'" (she is writing here of the metaphoric theme of a story which for her is the story of story) occurs, as in the moment in which a poet/poem appropriates/translates. The remembrance of this story of story takes place in a sequence in which H.D. recalls the perils of travel between the wars, during which she meditates upon the poetics of displacement, of having no "room," let alone a "Haus" like Freud and Goethe. Let us call this an allegory of American writing, or simply of writing in general, of reading, as it were, only in borrowed books: of writing always already in at least two languages, the poetic and the critical.

Chapter Three
Hart Crane and Hegel

I

We are all, unsuspectingly or not, Hegelians under the skin, even the so-called poststructural theorist, according to one of the most eminent of that genre.[1] For despite the poststructural or postmodern fracture of the book and the symbol, there would be no site for the parasites of contemporary theory without the "great Hegelian formulas," as Whitman called them, those large schemas for totalizing thought that organize and institutionalize intellectual life and at the same time offer the possibility of innovative and individual contretemps. But what kind of Hegelian or counter-Hegelian might we be, what kind of narrativist or counter-narrativist of the imagination? What kind of "Nietzsche in Basel" or "Lenin by the lake," to recall Wallace Stevens's lines from "Description without Place," might our modernist poets, or even we their "critics," assume as personae in order to read this Hegelianism, this modernity?

The notion of "Hegel in America" must appear a very arbitrary one, just as the idea of an American thought or the unity of our national consciousness is virtually unthinkable, especially in the context of an intellectual history that can refer confidently to the differences and oppositions of German and French thought, or employ such notions as those of a national or nativist language, or even of a certain kind of language that is the ground of a discipline. I am referring, of course, to the claims, virtually unchallenged from Kant to Heidegger, that German is the natural language of philosophy and French only one of its non-cognitive branches, of aesthetics, erotics, play. In this history, America, as Hegel himself forecast, is out of the game. "America," he proclaimed, in the Introduction to *The Philosophy of History*, is the beyond of history, some future site of history that is at the same time other than any history played out in Europe, the West: "It is the land of desire for all those who are weary of the historical lumber-room of Europe"; as the "Land of the Future," it is "only an echo of the Old World" up to the present moment, the nineteenth century which marks an end of history; and thus it stands beyond History with a capital "H" and is of no regard for philosophy, since philosophy's concern is with "neither past nor future" but with reason's or mind's destiny.[2]

"America" was, is, the kind of potentially new idea that Emerson and later Whitman tended to imagine and inscribe within the power of an act, we may say writing, that would in turn invent an astonishingly new "America." And Whitman, if not Emerson, showed little or no knowledge of Hegel—Whitman claimed to find the key to the "new," the idea of democracy, in what little of the German he read, which does not seem to include *The Philosophy of History*. In Whitman's view, based on a most limited series of Hegelian texts, these formulas manifest the broadest and most comprehensive expression of the democratic self as power, though as we will see, in his poems there are ever intensifying glimpses of this self's limit and undoing. Without examining too closely Hegel's mode of articulating individual (finite) and collective consciousness in the metaphors of "family romance" or genealogy, Whitman was quick to grasp in the general systematics of Hegelian formulas the notion of an interplay between force and form, act and idea, that would allow the "poet of the modern" to overcome his belatedness and his bad conscience, and to reclaim his agency, his inventive potency—or in other words, to make it new in repetition.

Out of this appropriation of the Hegelian idea, and in the name of the democratic, the poet could refashion a genetic myth, in the name of America and the "Me-myself." His poem, as literal corpus of the self, would be at once the book and the agent of history, the actualization of force and the advent of the modern—in sum, what Pound would call "ideas into action." Thus Whitman in a sense inaugurates the rewriting of genetic myths as myths of originary displacement, beginning again. And this partial reading, or inevitable misreading, of Hegel makes the Whitmanesque poem/poetic into a trope of the very mythogemes and mythothemes it has itself originarily, as it were, re-*fashioned* (redressed) out of philosophy or philosophemes. That is, the Whitman mythos, the figure of the self embodied and the body as cosmos, becomes in the tropological fashioning of the poem a notion of consciousness as symbol, but a symbol which repeatedly undoes itself in the history of its becoming. The figure a poem makes foreshadows its own undoing or self-overcoming. A poem/figure, after Whitman's fashion, a poem of the future, a democratic poem, can neither be nor mean. It can only do.

But rather than examining the political implications and contradictions of Whitman's democratic poetics, I would like to concentrate here on what is at stake in his claim for a poem of the future for which there is no present poem, only a prefiguration, as it were.[3] We might recall that as late as "Democratic Vistas" he was calling for this poem of the future, this realized democracy which was not yet realized, even in his own sublime prefigurations or "Leaves" of the book. The poem of the future, that is, could only appear in a poem anterior to it, a poem in the act of inventing it, and thus a poem of history that was autogenetic. In American poetics, from Emerson to Wallace Stevens and beyond, this poem would be like a "giant on the horizon" (Stevens, "A Primitive Like an Orb") and "patron of origins," and thus a revisionary figure of the sublime. It is as if every poet had to invent America as future anew, and prefigure it as a trope. Like Emerson's horizonal literature in the essay "Circles," which gives us purchase in our "hodiernal circle" in order to see further circles, this poem would also forecast or throw forward. This poem would be some new kind of sublime, not an awesome and uncognizable figuration that heralds the universal by marking its own limit or blinding the "transparent eyeball," but a figure marking its own ultimate sublation and death. For while Hegel's theory of art anticipates a future in which the Spirit overcomes its phenomenal fate, or philosophy displaces poetry, the American (and democratic) poem seems to imagine its sacrifice as the sacrifice of the father to his own second coming or second childhood—a kind of genealogical auto-production in which the figure tropes itself, prefigures by disfiguring, and thus marks itself as the origin of representation and not the presentation of origin. As Stevens writes of contradiction in "Connoisseur of Chaos," the poem will offer "Pages of illustrations," but the "luster" will be its own artful performance or tropology. Much like an essay.

II

In his essay "Circles," Emerson sets out to amplify, or indeed supplement, the titular figure which he calls the "highest emblem in the cipher of the world," the figure of metaphysics, ontotheology, of God, but also of figure itself: "emblem" and "cipher."[4] And the inquiry, if it is that, or elaboration soon turns up a problematic. The figure Emerson addresses has already been drawn, or redrawn, in a poem that serves as epigraph. It is Emerson's poem, his particular signature or "emblem" of a totality he has already overwritten while underwriting it as the "highest." The circle is not one cipher among others; it cannot be reduced or partitioned, yet it is also a part, a synecdoche, of the whole, and a part of a part, an emblem of the eye and of the I. The eye forms the first circle, just as an I or finite consciousness may form the first poem, the Idea's emblem. For if the circle, as Emerson cites St. Augustine's adage of the form "whose center was everywhere and its circumference nowhere," is an emblem, and the eye both one of its manifestations and its genesis, then the origin is always already a trope. "A new genesis were here," as the poem/epigraph puts it—the poem being Emerson's own composition that forms the textual genesis of his essay, a work in turn originating itself out of the Augustine text (II, 301–2).

The essay, then, stages its own production as an act of reading, as a "circular and compensatory" troping of the circle's "copious sense" into a yet larger sense. This decentering of origin by repetition, of the first by the second, of center by circumference or horizon, marks an Emersonian displacement of perfection (the "Unattainable") by power. For many readers of

Emerson, this is the first act or gesture of a new humanism, of positioning the central man. But in its displacement of nature (symbol of God in his phenomena) by man (eye, I) or the proper by the figural, man appears as the name of his generic act. He appears as trope, a center precipitated upon the horizon, outside of our hodiernal circle. The new center is named the poet, a son replacing the father. The poet/son is like the philosopher, a reader and troper of a pre-text: Aristotle platonized; man not only realizes but adds, like the various actors—poets, lovers, and so on—of Stevens's "A Primitive Like an Orb" (440) who constantly rewrite the "giant on the horizon" by a kind of tropological supplementation.

Emerson thus nominates himself, both as poet and as literature itself, as an "experimenter" that projects by quotation. To recall both an earlier essay, *Nature*, and a later one, "Quotation and Originality," both of which I have commented on at length elsewhere, we might note that this positioning of literature and maker on the verge or horizon, anticipates or repeats in a curious way the structure of the family romance of Hegel which Derrida reads in *Glas*. Just as language, the sign, as sublated things, "in the sign, the signifier (exterior) is sublated by signification, by the signified sense (ideal), the *Bedeutung*, the concept. The concept sublates the sign which sublates the thing. The signified sublates the signifier which sublates the referent."[5] This produces what Derrida calls a "dialectophage" or murder of the sign, a destruction of natural language: "Natural language bears and touches in itself the sign of death," and its cadaver is resurrected in the concept (philosophy), just as the son must be sacrificed (murdered) in Spirit's fulfillment of its *telos*, and, by extension, poetry must experience its death in the service of philosophy.

But Emerson's (almost) parody of Hegel, his mimicry of this "dialectophage," becomes a strategic intervention, allowing poetry to displace philosophy, and the son the father. Poetry does not annul philosophy, but resurrects itself by quotation, reinscribing the idea in the act, the sign as both signified and signifier in the trope's turning, its circle. The eye/I becomes the horizonal position literally in its turn.

Literature's belatedness becomes a strange earliness. One

might read into this a kind of allegory of what American literature might be, as originary quotation. Whitman's advertisements for himself are only indices to the thematic redundancy of claiming originality while at the same time regretting that the original and yet modern poem has not yet been written. In "Democratic Vistas," for example, long after the almost virginal appearance of "Song of Myself" has issued in revisions and elaboration of a developing *Leaves*, the Bard still announces that we are only on the verge of the truly modern and democratic poem. And like Emerson's verge, its figure remains the tropologically embodied I, the eye in and out of the body, the referent sublated in the sign and the sign (corporeal signifier) as the provisional sign for and wound of the idea.

This is the figure of Emerson's *Nature*, the notoriously overdetermined "transparent eyeball" which is misread, I believe, as a simple emblem of unmediated vision (I, 8–10). Because Emerson situates his figure not at a transcendental center but in a "bare common" or even "in the woods" or upon a "bare ground" or "wilderness," that is, an horizontal landscape which it organizes as "part and parcel of God," the self is effaced in the emblem of the eye. This poet's eye and I are figural, synecdochal, part and parcel, a reading borne out in the essay's conclusion which evokes the figure of man as a "god in ruins" and the poet as self-redemptive man. The poem, the poetic I, includes "both history and prophet." It repairs the axial law that should align vision and things, that law which has become a "ruin or blank" for contemporary man (I, 72–73). Disunited within himself, suffering from an opaque eye rather than transparency, man has become like Hegel's finite consciousness. But in the poem it remains possible to "behold the real higher law" once again, even though the poem remains figural, historical as well as prophetic.

The "new center," Emerson had written in *Nature*, is prospective, the "verge of today," not an origin but a "patron of origin" as in Stevens's poem, and thus pre-original. The "concentrum" of the poem is a figural prophecy of a unity to be, but as Stevens's poem reads it, the poem is a "fated eccentricity." The "giant" of writing is overdetermined, a "skeleton of the ether," and a figure "ever changing." As "tenacious particle," it is a synecdoche, but only of some possible and futural "central poem" (440–43). The "patron" on the "horizon" centers the origin eccentrically in its tropological maneuvers, revealing how each rewriting is a reading of an earlier figure as if it were later, and the anticipation of a later figure inscribes both past and future within itself, its double writing, just as Stevens's poem may be said to read the eccentric and prophetic role that Emerson makes the poem play in his essay.

III

Stevens's poem allows us to read Emerson's positioning of the poem, of figural language, on the verge as a situating of trope at the "new center." Just as Whitman would read the Emersonian prophecy of the poem/figure as a self-engendering (and even auto-inseminating) trope. It is what Whitman celebrates as "Nature without check with original energy," a nature centered in the corporeal I which celebrates itself and sings itself. Celebrating and singing the self (oneself), however, is not a simple notion, and its conditions would produce some extreme transformations from "Song of Myself" to the *Sea Drift* poems, conditions that can tell us something about the economy of self-reflective performances. Quite simply, to "celebrate" oneself requires the conditions of undoing an old self with each utterance that adds to or enlarges the self; so that the self in saying I falls victim to the conditions of unfolding that Hegel engages when he examines what is entailed in the I saying "I." "With the twirl of my tongue I encompass worlds and volumes of worlds," Whitman writes in "Song of Myself," but like Melville in *Moby Dick*, to encompass old "volumes" is to quote a nature and be transformed in it.[6]

We might recall Paul de Man's analysis of the Hegelian utterance "When I say I," that leads to yet another kind of utterance according to de Man: "I cannot say I" ("Sign and Symbol," 768). Though it is impossible here to summarize the ironic rigor of de Man's reading, it is necessary to point out that he begins it by tying Hegel's ontology to his aesthetics, specifically to his distinction between sign and symbol, and by arguing that contrary to familiar notions, Hegel's apparent privileging of the symbol over the sign leads to a problematical impasse or *aporia* in his efforts to write the history of consciousness. De Man's startling linkage of aesthetics and history turns on Hegel's contradictory notion of the sign's arbitrariness and phenomenality, its degradation on the one hand, and its freedom from determination or its free function on the other, in contrast to the symbol's phenomenal inscription as a signified. Out of this apparent but not symmetrical contradiction, de Man notices and remarks Hegel's double stress on the I as sign and sign-producing, that is, on the nature and stature of the "grammatical subject" which realizes itself with a certain predicative freedom. Just as the symbol is at once reified and determined in perception, the perceptual I would be entombed in its body or phenomena; but the grammatical I, in its saying or performance, *would be*, in a certain sense, *free* even of its own determinations. Like Emerson's over celebrated figure of "Man Thinking," the Hegelian I or grammatical subject lives at risk of its freedom.

Now, one hesitates to pull back from the abstractive formulas of Hegel, that move between stable concepts and performative overdetermination, to poetic performances upon which such already overwrought figures as the tropic I depends. First, as Hegel notices, the characteristic of thought, of thinking as manifest in sign, is abstraction, or increasing abstraction—repetition as generalization. Thus the I as grammatical subject is a generalized/generalizing I, and not the reference to an essential or privative subject; an I, therefore, that stands for all selves in relation to the other. "The philosophical I," writes de Man, and we might add here the poetic I, the I which speaks volumes, "is not only self-effacing, as Aristotle demanded, in the sense of being humble and inconspicuous, it is also self-effacing in the much more radical sense that the position of the I, which is the condition for thought, implies its eradication . . . as the undoing, the erasure of any relationship, logical or otherwise, that could be conceived between what the I is and what it says it is" ("Sign and Symbol," 768—69). This I which says/thinks is a sign rather than a symbol, and can be represented only by a linguistic position. Perhaps the most startling formulation of its position is Peirce's apothegmic declaration that "man is a sign," at once representation and interpretation. We should not forget what this irresistible self-effacement meant for Emerson and for Whitman, threatened as they were by the role thrust upon them as representative men in a democratic world where all representations were equal and anonymous, like Hegel's "abstract generality."

For as soon as Whitman conceives (almost literally) himself as democratic poet speaking "volumes of worlds," he must confront the end of any dream of transparency or reflexive identity. The poet in his freedom was subject to the "velocity" of change, of self-effacement, which also involved effacing those worlds he had "encompassed," nature or other texts, in order to translate and sublate them. While every poet finds himself already inscribed in the "printed and bound book," he must speak yet other volumes. For "He most honors my style who learns under it to destroy the teacher," a sentiment echoed nearly a century later in Williams's *Paterson*, a poem dedicated to effacing the Europeanized or western subject, the father (Pater) language, in order to free the son to father a new world language.

The problem, however, is not the inevitability of this succession or displacement, this genealogy, but its ever-increasing speed, what Whitman calls its velocity. The velocities of change overwhelm self-reflection, and accentuate its eccentricity or liminality, its representations, that is, the disfigurement and death of the self transacted in the subject's thinking. There is perhaps no more vivid a figure of the displaced middle of American poetics than the one which organizes the scene of self-reading in Whitman's "As I Ebb'd with the Ocean of Life," one of the two canonical *Sea Drift* poems and first titled "Bardic Symbols." The poem's scene is, to echo Emerson, a "verge," a liminal "ebbing" of the "electric self" who discovers that his very act of creation, of writing, is a death (254). But it is death in a strange and unfamilial sense. First, there is no scene of instruction here, no handing on of the mantle from father to son; nor even a scene of displacement. But rather, we are witness to a massive undoing of any such genealogical drama of telic violence. Second, the poem graphically portrays writing as an act of reflective effacement (the poet walking upon the "shores I know. . . seeking types" but finding no self-representations) that annuls the poet's essential or symbolic nature. Reflection upon these driftworks reveals no origin either of them, as natural objects, or of the poetic self. Like the hieroglyphic bones of Hart Crane's "At Melville's Tomb," these obscure signs cannot be read as the poet wishes: that is, as reflections or representations of himself. They are neither synecdochal nor symbolic, but graphic signs (like Crane's "vivid hieroglyphs") provoking interpretation, demanding to be read. The poet discovers himself as only another of the pieces of detritus, as a reader reading. Nothing is a type, or belongs to a typological order; nothing reflects its origin or reveals direction, neither "sands" (and one remembers Blake's figure) nor "dead leaves" (possibly Whitman's own poetic leavings). In sum, what one might hope to be a readable or symbolic world is effaced. There is no revelation, and the face of things, resisting a reading, interfering with self-reflection, becomes the sign of the self's undoing, its death. The poet's acts of reflection, of thought, entail his own effacement. The returning objects or signs compose a dirge of his own thinking/reading. It is as if all the poems of the world pass before his eyes, drift up in his memory, but from what direction?

And the question of direction, of *telos*, is crucial, since all questions of the future seem questions of direction. But drift, as we know, is a modern problem, in which the innuendo of teleology is subject to redundancy and overdetermination. With this gesture, and others in the *Sea Drift* poems, Whitman annuls once and for all the illusion of a symbolic or reflexive world, and makes indelible the flaws or marks of contradiction that had been so artfully (rhetorically) concealed in Emerson's false dialectic of the way one might build a metaphoric house or American genealogy out of driftworks or quotations. Hence, Whitman must submit his own translative poem to a deconstruction which turns out to be a commentary on its difficulties in catching the drift of what has come before his eyes.

For these signs are not symbols, and will not reflect him. Instead, he repeats them in a kind of reading. There is a similar scene in the other canonical *Sea Drift* poem, "Out of the Cradle Endlessly Rocking," in which the divided I of the poet serves as a kind of translating song, hearing and interpreting a division, a "he-bird" and "she-bird" who can be united only as a "thousand warbling echoes" that might be gleaned in the utterance of the former (252). But the utterance of the he-bird is only heard as echoes, because of the silence or absence of the former, that is, of death, the name of absence which is also the word. The word includes, inscribes death, but no longer in the presence-absence, self-other opposition, and the poem develops in terms of, in the regard of, a self who in translating this scene is translated by it. The fate of the poet, the subject, the translator lies in the time, the tempo, of his reading translation. Whitman writes on the verge of the modern, of the modern as verge. Its theme, as Henry Adams knew, was speed or velocity, turning or trope rather than representation. In Emerson's terms, it will be not the figure of "representative Man" so much as "Man Thinking," and for Whitman it will mandate an effacement of the self in the body or death.

Whitman had discovered in "Song of Myself" that even to sing and celebrate the self was to augment and enlarge it, to increase the body's mass so as to encompass the "en-masse." But this growing sublimity tended not to regulate the axiological and analogical relation between finite and universal consciousness, or between the natural and transcendental, with Emersonian transparency. The scene of translation performed in "Out of the Cradle" and "As I Ebb'd" would have to reflect on the obdurate figure of the body/poem which undoes all such hopes for the word and for the possibility of anthropocentric literature. If Whitman begins by evoking something like Kant's figure of the sublime colossus in the "Third Critique," in which the human body and language regulate what Wallace Stevens calls the "effects of analogy," the movement between natural and transcendental, he will have to conclude with a rather more despairing vision of vision, in which the figure of the sublime obscures the sun with its shadow. In Whitman, music signifies the law of nature's order, just as the poem as music orders and catalogues the manifold and multitudes. The words or drifts of the later poems, which are no less revisionary translations of the earlier, disperse the celebrated man/center and precipitate it upon the horizon: as in "On the Beach at Night

Alone" (260–61), the "I think[s] a thought of the clef of the universes and of the future," the "clef" being both break and dividing musical notation or sign. While the poet still desires to enclose the "vast similitudes" in the "All" of his utterance, while he wants not only to declare but to regulate the purpose and direction of nature, as center dispatched to the verge or margin, this I (which no longer sees) can speak only as one of the fragments or atoms which proceed in "motley procession" ("After the Sea-Ship," 263).

Man is no longer the measure, nor the poem an adequate place or agent. The poem is no longer an adequate presentation of the unpresentable, but more importantly, must reflect the inadequacy of itself as presentation. The poem can no longer serve as bridge and symbol, but rather announces the strange effects of another economy (an "economimesis," one might say, of aesthetics, of taste, of repetition, of undoing). The poem/word/I on the shore/margin/horizon can only reflect on itself, its marginality. Yet, as decentered and eccentric, the poem does reflect the contradictions of self-reflection. Like the detritus washing up on the sands in "As I Ebb'd" (a poem first entitled "Bardic Symbols"), old poems and figures return and are turned in the new poem's reflections, revealing that these new reflections are echoes, like the "thousand warbling echoes" of the poet's song in "Out of the Cradle." The poem reveals that this song, which is a translation, bears within itself the word "death." The word is at once death and the "word death." It has become a sign, but a thinking or grammatical sign marking the destiny of the I (252–53).

It is within this scene that Whitman begins to rethink the idea of America or the great democratic poem as a poem always already horizontal, a future-present, and hence inadequate presentation. This poem, then, will be adequate, but only "ages hence," and then only in the writings of "recorders" who take instruction from present inscriptions: "I will tell you what to say of me" (see both "Recorders Ages Hence" and "Inscriptions," 121, 1). Present poems offer a "profound lesson of reception" ("Song of the Open Road," 150), but like Peirce's sign inscribe the necessity of their own interpretation. The American poet is fated to write this poem endlessly. That Whitman chooses to enact this scene of reading/instruction within poems like "As I Ebb'd" as a scene of death indicates his apprehension over the major problematics of the modern.

This may perhaps help explain why American writers in general, and particularly those who were so preoccupied not only with personal identity but with the task of impersonally representing the nation, of engendering a national identity and language, found literature to be a better instrument for thinking than philosophy. For literature could mark the strategies of *making*, of invention and self-invention, as prospective more than self-reflective. Having no history or tradition to determine representation, the American poet would be enslaved to a false "patron of origins" unless he or she could make the last first, the repetition originary, and the act of recording a translation. The modern poem, then, or Emerson's threshold literature, would have to function with the prospective force of trope, rather than reveal the imminence of symbol. An American poetics of the sublime could not be, as Stevens recorded in the first canto of "Esthetique du Mal," the sublime in the old sense, making "sure of the most correct catastrophe," but a sublime revealing the undoing of the book of the sublime. This poem will mime its own undoing and translation, not its failure but rather its questioning of the sublime perfection which constitutes all human efforts as ulitmate failures. It is thus a rejection of the very poem as symbol that the poet sets out to realize.

Crane, indeed, is an exceptional case of the modernist crisis which one can find in poets as different as Stevens and Pound—exceptional perhaps only in the anxiety he evidences over the indirectness of language and thus the motives for metaphor. While Pound and so-called objectivist poetics in general found the Image (its aesthetic, phenomenal, and even natural status) preferable to the symbol and indeed prior to it, and found in symbolism a move away from the precision and historicity of originary poetic language; and while Stevens revels in the productive irony of a "world of words" spun out of the "act of the mind," Crane seems almost paralyzed by the double-bind of the poem which remains a cryptic symbol. Compare his famous (or infamous) claims for the "logic of metaphor" and his argument that the poet generates a new "single word" out of some alembic of the words at his disposal with, on the one hand, Pound's argument, following Fenollosa's notes, that all poetic language is metaphoric or translative, transferential, thus natural, or, on the other, Stevens's insistence upon a fictive reality, a "realm of resemblance" that we recognize to be fictive and thus a human construct, cultural and not natural. The question of the word, of what experimental modernism heralded as the "revolution of the word," always arises in the place that Derrida calls the "tain" of the mirror, the position of reflection. It is situated at precisely the "point" (Derrida would emphasize the French double sense of the noun position and the adverbial negation, not exact opposites) where the poet/poem is forced to reflect upon itself. The point, that point, is what is called modernism.

What attracts us to Crane, then, is not his anxious and essentially sublimated preoccupation with the aesthetic symbol, but the effects of his trying to produce it and thus the effects of his reflections upon the status and stature of the word—the erection of the word, as in "The Broken Tower," and its undoing in the tolling (as in the Derridean *"glas"*) of the "broken" poem. It is a question, as the poem phrases it, not of cognition but of the cognate:

> My word I poured. But was it cognate, scored
> Of that tribunal monarch of the air
> Whose thigh embronzes earth, strikes crystal Word
> In wounds pledged once to hope—cleft to despair?[7]

The tolling and mourning of the word, its cleft and clef, and thus its flawed nature, situates it in that middle place that Kant saw for the aesthetic, where it is not cognitive but might be a fulcrum or bridge between phenomenal and noumenal. Crane's word reverberates the questionable nature of the Word incarnate, of the poem as disfigured and fallen body—of the poem as fallen erection which is no longer central. The poem undoes itself in self-mourning. Again, as in Whitman, the musical clef and the cleft of writing mingle to disturb the meditation of the poem/word upon itself, leaving the body of the Word, the poet's body, in fragments.

The poet's eye, his emblem of the "visionary company of love" (135), is now drawn to that which does not exactly reflect him, or drawn to mediate between finite and universal consciousness. He cannot decide whether it is himself as symbol or a technical construct, a sign. He cannot read himself. This reinscription (probably unconscious) of Hegel's notion of the symbol and the sublime into the problematics of modernism begins to reflect modernism's undoing at its so-called origins. Hegel's writing already predicated the turn toward language. First, recall the famous definition of the symbol in his *Lectures on Aesthetics*, the symbol as a unity divided within itself, at once prior to the sign but also of the sign, a kind of sublation of the sign, yet grounded literally or at least phenomenally in the sign.[8] This symbol is, as Paul de Man observed, a synecdoche; but as part of a whole, the universal, it is also an arbitrary part or kind of radical fragment. It is thus a kind of synecdoche of synecdoche.

Symbolic art, as Hegel subsequently argues, must inevitably be involved in the question of the symbol's sublimity, its being unreadable because it is the "beginning of art" or the "threshold of art," belonging to the East, yet prima facie a sign and a mark of that death necessary for the transit of spirit through the West. Taking up the Kantian distinction between the beautiful and the sublime in the *Critique of Judgement*, Hegel extrapolates the Kantian effort to situate (the figure of) man. And, thus, as we have seen, consciousness or the I becomes a notion of the sign's freedom or action, the movement toward law and generalization manifest in the grammatical I, through the sign's self-nullification. The sign is both repetitive (it submits to an "inner obedience") and resistant (it manifests a "stubbornness against the law"), giving it, as we will see, a critical as well as aesthetic status.

What Hegel calls in a chapter title the "Conscious Symbolism of the Comparative Art Form" (378 ff.) evidences the peculiar role of sublimity and symbolism, in which one must consider the symbol both as work and working, as both thing and act. For "conscious symbolism" (and it serves Hegel as a kind of name for modernism, or at least for the threshold of the modern, though it belongs to ancient, glyphic art or writing), marks its difference from "unconscious symbolism" in its marked "*non-correspondence*" or separation of meaning, explicitly known in its inwardness, and the concrete appearance divided therefrom. This separation and hierarchization of meaning and particularity, of the universal and its representation, is the irreducible signature of the sublime, and cannot be repaired. In the "subjective activity of the poet," the relation of the two is always characterized as a "more or less accidental concatenation," so that the figure of the sublime always appears as a "cognate spiritual meaning" in which the marks of separation and degradation can never be effaced. Thus the "determinate or restricted meaning" (the phenomenal representation) comes to displace the priority of the Absolute (the concept, the content). In terms of the earlier distinction between the sign and the symbol that is also prima facie a sign, the particularity (or negativity of the concept) of the work, its figurality, is at once de-privileged and reinscribed in its priority. Its fallenness, its historicity, its didacticism becomes a kind of ironic firstness, as a Peircean might say.

The recalcitrance of the symbolic is essentially for Hegel the limits of language, marking the unbridgeable abyss between figure and concept. But it also centralizes the marginality of the abyss whose figure is the bridge, figure itself. At once natural and spiritual, or uncertain conjunction of the two, the "symbolic and comparative art-form" never quite overcomes the duality of separation and conjunction that signifies the historical economy of the West. Hegel's literary or art history, which is also an allegory of the history of Spirit, unfolds dialectially from East to West, and from the Symbolic to the Classical to the Romantic, but always in terms of the ratio between ideal content and phenomenal form. Spirit is repeatedly drawn through the beautiful (the material and sensuous) and never quite manages to escape the drag of its objectivity. In its sublime and sublimated stages, its symbolic form can only hint at the subjective overcoming or the sublative moment in which its determinations and yet its freedom (as sign) is returned to itself. Thus the history that also unfolds from the many to one, from pantheism to monotheism, and from representation to expression, even finally from the tentative balances and unity of form-content in

classical art to the death of the naturalized spirit and finite consciousness in the romantic, can only be seen as an arc of the circle, the negation of negativity. For the romantic can never quite
throw off the face of this negation (the prima facie beauty and
health of the classical sign), this tragic mask of death as the
mother of beauty, and thus reveals the ugly contingency, the
phenomenality of degradation that spirit must pass through.
Hegel calls this the "genuine phoenix-life of spirit," which includes forms of its dissolution—like Poe's forms of the
grotesque and arabesque.

However formulated, this Hegelian art history can never ex-
tract the concept from its figuration (and disfiguration). Philosophy, as he says, always has its Good Friday, but reflected in
the religious revelations of the romantic art-form which never
finally sublates, overcomes, or transcends its representations,
however effectively it outlives and effaces the "graven images"
of pantheism with its visage of the divine man. If the Hegelian
story brings us to the threshold of the Spirit's return, its turn toward and into itself through the finite consciousness and its
grammatical tendency toward generalization, it also brings us
to an impasse or impassable horizon, the modern, where the
old crisis of "symbolic and comparative art-form," the symbol as
sublime sign, is redoubled. The return of the symbol as construct, as technical or unnatural erection, reintroduces the
question of representation and negation in terms of a new thematic, of dynamism and power rather than genealogy, so that
the determining phenomenality of the figural form, of language, is reinscribed as problematical. In other words, Hegel
brings us through self-reflection to the impasses of reflection
upon reflection, to what Derrida calls the chiasmatic moment
of dissemination.

The problematic status of art, of the poem as conscious symbol, fills the entire history of the West, like a bridge, and cannot
be effaced or repressed by the expressive disfigurations of the
Romantic. Modernism, in the guises of romantic art, rehearses
that history, in the drama of art's displacement of religion. But
this ensures that the work of this art-form will appear not as a
representation or expression of spirit, or even of the idea of
man, but as a technical construction signifying the idea of the

natural/organic. Hegel's romantic pathos anticipates its modernist deconstruction, in which the technical erection not only represents the organic, the idea of nature, but serves as its pseudo-origin. Just as in the later Heidegger, where the bridge does not so much provide transit over the abyss as it defines the form of the abyss, otherwise formless, the Hegelian symbol, which is also irreducibly a sign, indicates in its repetitive nature the priority and originarity of figurality.

For modernism the metaphor of performance and action, what Stevens called the "poem of the act of the mind" and Pound named in the dynamics of the moving Image, later Vortex, displaces the immanence of the symbol, in a manner that can only reveal that the symbol is always already a symbol of the symbol or of the sublime. What Lyotard calls the modernist sublime, or modernism as a poetics of the sublime, subsists in the Janus-faced symbol that averts reflection, that resists self-reflection. The act of the modern poem is less reflexive, and genetic, than a productive act of self-reading. In its attempt to legitimate itself, to reify itself as symbol, the poem tropes itself or produces a set (a tropological series) of effects, of quotations, like those which Pound found in Maletesta's "post-bag" (or the "rag-bag" with which he began an early version of Canto Two) or Tempio; or even the Thesaurus of Canto IV which remains the genetic source that will conclude in the acknowledged incoherence of the "palimpsest" of Canto CXVI, which asks who will read it, or who, in the Peircean sense, will marks its necessity as "interpretant" sign. The Stevensian "and yet(s)" of his "never-ending meditation" in "An Ordinary Evening in New Haven" compose another rhetorical version, and a different kind of poetry perhaps, of this modernist confrontation with what Williams called the "edge" of the image, the glyphic and graphic sign, the poem as a word that marks its limit, its own margin.

IV

Hart Crane's poetry might seem to offer, as we have noted, an exception (a sublime one) to this paradoxically affirmative and productive celebration of the modernist Image as glyph or graphic resistance to self-reflexivity. His "logic of metaphor" and his confrontation with the "livid hieroglyphics" ("At Melville's Tomb," 100) posed by all old texts, in this particular case with the American versions or reinscriptions and thus readings of a past that cannot be its origin, might provide us with a scene of modernism. His attempt to write an American or literary epic in *The Bridge*, to engender, as he claimed, a poem that would be a "new word" which the reader would recognize when he "left it" or, presumably, finished with his reading-interpretation, could very well provide us with what Heidegger might call the technical impasses of modernism.

In his effort to appropriate and then reverse the very dynamics that have replaced the unitary force of the *logos*, Crane is forced to redraft a poetics of the margin or the sublime, of the symbolic as a failure, into a poetics of what Henry Adams called the "dynamo." One way of following out what Crane asserts as the uncanny "logic of metaphor," his word for the poem as "new word," might be an exploration of his misreading of a text that had an inordinate if perverse effect on early American modernism—Spengler's *Decline of the West*.[9] But this cannot be done as a history of ideas, of nihilism, in the manner of many studies of poetic derivation from philosophy. Indeed, Crane's and Eliot's mutual if opposed uses of Spengler's metaphysical narrative (more Hegelian than Nietzschean, one might argue) is in itself one of the curious if affirmative instances of (mis-)interpretative violence within modernism: Crane's forced optimism set against Eliot's echoes of Spengler's pessimistic critique of the modern. Eliot, of course, accepted what Spengler described as decline, and authored a move to redeem this plight of spiritual history; in this he repeats Hegel's ontotheology even as he rejects Romanticism. Crane, on the other hand, chose to misread or trope declination, to skew it, to produce *askesis*, as it were. Recent studies of Crane, most significantly John Irwin's study of the uses of "perspectivism" in the panelling of *The Bridge*'s unfolding structure, have enforced this Cranian reading of Spengler's negative theology.[10] Irwin reveals the haunting and even perverse function of perspective in any aesthetics that is centered upon the economy of specularity, for perspective is clearly (a strange word here) a notion of resistance and power, an interpretive effort to preserve an individual or communal entity, and thus an historical act.

At stake in Crane's anti-Eliot reading of Spengler, as Irwin speculates, is a problem of the sublime, of *trans*lating the eternal into a history that represents it as spectacle. It is a problem of the image and of the imaginative, and of the "marge" which must be negotiated in any act of translation—like that of Leonardo's translation of Biblical revelation into spatial narrative or Crane's retranslation of history and its perspectives (including the literary texts of America) back into some verbum res of the poem. Irwin focuses on the task of the translation assumed by Leonardo in his Sistine narrative, a problem of perspectivity in recounting a narrative cycle within the spatial enclosures of a single room (the task of sanctification along with that of closing an enclosure). In Spengler's narrative, the artist is a Faustian figure willing to lose himself in accumulation of power; and he marks, in a certain way, the modernist's logical conclusion of post-classical culture.

Irwin recounts Spengler's argument for a cultural history derived from a history of art that has to engage the question of temporality in spatial terms, and the efforts of artists to find between the classical figure of the naked human body and the modernist or Faustian world of polyphonic music, some "third dimension" or resolution of the time-space dilemma. Crane, he argues, under the influence of Spengler, is motivated to think out the modern poet's dilemma in terms of this space-time, visual art/polyphonic music dialectic, with the poet cast in the role of Faustian subject whose perspective of individual will centralizes without resolving the struggle. It is my contention that Crane is or becomes less a Spenglerean than he appears, and simply because he has to confront all the problems of self-reflexive ordering, and thus of the symbol, opened up by Hegel and aggravated by Nietzsche. We find this tension worked out in Crane's attempt to resolve the position of the poetic self, the poem, and the word, or poetic language in general.

This is the condition of Crane's *Bridge*, both figure and poem. The poet aspires to reify its title, and thus itself as genetic figure—the bridge, and hence the abyss it covers, as origin and end—while at the same time affirming its priority to either origin or end. As *logos*, or new word, it reveals itself in the poet's gaze as only a trope at the threshold. It reveals the trope of the center to be only a technical construction, a "Paradigm" of the center on the horizon, which like the figure of the colossus in Kant can never quite be read by the one who conceived it as "Paradigm" or "Verb." And the abyss it bridges (ocean or oceanic force; river or entropic manifestation of that force's unilinear and irreversible direction which the poet desires to see flowing back into itself) becomes a threshold center, precipitating the poet as reader into its shadow. This is the complicated and problematic issue of poetic space Crane encounters in trying to conceive the poem as "new word."

Crane's figure of the bridge, then, is not an immanent figure but a graphic one, one to which he gives names derived from language—the Bridge as both noun and verb, subject and predicate. It does not organize within itself the moment of spirit's self-reflection or return, but motivates the poet's acts of reading, his efforts to find hints of the transcendental in the signs of a history: signs that have flowed under and across it, through it, and are perhaps sublated in it, as in proper names and metonyms. The bridge as symbol is also a sign, of chiasmatic crossings that everywhere mark the limit of vision in the sublimity of representation. And the poet, who wants to find himself reflected in this Verb finds himself, as finite consciousness, initially exiled from it. And further, neither he nor it is at the center.

Let us try to follow out the historical logic of Crane's installation of the bridge, his attempt to resurrect from the erection the power of its conception. First, Brooklyn Bridge is a modern technical miracle, a product not of mechanics but of dynamics, thus signifying a new spatial organization of time, a new sense of bridging. Second, Crane conceives it as a metonymy for the position of America in world history, as the place of the dream of opening up again a closed history of the West, of restoring the circle beyond the old teleological dream of manifest destiny. Connecting the lost Atlantis with Cathay, the bridge as symbol also doubles for the American continent as phenomenal connective, or Spirit's historical state of sublation. Yet the continent also bears within its geography a double mark of history: transcontinental railroad and macadam highway ("From Far Rockaway to Golden Gate") crosses in one direction the movement of another river, the Mississippi, just as the Bridge crosses the East River which links oceanic force with continental mass. The bridge, then, is not a fixed and sublime symbol but a master trope, turning under the poet's gaze like the enigma of a threshold that has occulted the transcendental. The bridge is not stable but turning, as the poet sees it, not a Virgin but a Dynamo "of the fury fused," as Henry Adams put it.

Crane's poem, however, takes its representative model not from the material bridge but from the modern graphic design of Joseph Stella which is an undoing of representation, or a representation of dynamics, of troping. For Stella's painting is a non-perspectival rendering of Roebling's dynamic (and Hegelian) idea of the dialectical bridge.[11] Wherever the poet as finite consciousness turns he must confront the enigma of a turning stability. He is drawn to it as (if he is) a part of it, seeking his reflection in it. But all he discovers is that it is refractive rather than reflective. As paradigm it will not be conjugated under his control, but marks the abyss between figure and any possible transcendental. The bridge as poem/symbol is not only part ("arc"), rather than whole ("circle"), it is not simply unreadable, but it signifies further the aberrations of the poet's desire to master it, to translate it (the "word") as other in his image ("new word"). The bridge as figure tropes the poet, abysses him, and marks his anonymity as "pariah." Like Whitman's democratic self, or Emily Dickinson's diminished self, he becomes everybody and nobody, reflected in and by everything, and reflecting nothing.

Crane's poet becomes the poem/bridge, then, in a disincarnation of the word, being consumed by his work: he is at once self-consumed and consumed by the other. Simple sublation is suspended and the self is disseminated like the atoms of a democratic nation in every direction, to be gathered up into nuclei or multi-centers that suggest a new sense of history. America is not a mythos or a history of repetition, any more than one can find in it, as Eliot sought and thought he found in Judeo-Christian history and in pagan mythology, a pattern that legitimated and reified the circle. Crane's poet, precipitated beneath the arc of the circle, finds himself turning within its turnings (see the "Proem"), reading that which curves back upon itself not as past but as some kind of future anterior. The future consumes him, consumes the past. Just as Columbus was consumed by an anticipated discovery he could not possess, and was possessed by it even as he tried to name it in borrowed (proper) names, Melville, Whitman, Dickinson, Isadora Duncan, and Poe, among others, have been consumed; only to reappear in the misty figurations of their culture's history as the ignored spokes(wo)men of that culture, metonyms of a culture that exiles them. In *The Bridge*, they compose a metonymic history of the true but suppressed representatives of the history, because their representations interdict the idea of America's continuity with the West. As performers, they signify America's decentered and decentering role—the role of exile—in the history of the West (ontotheology).

Crane's poem confesses, in a sense, that the only America it can envision is nothing more than what was originally nothing other than a represented vision, a representation that precedes the ideal it represents. The representation preceded any presentation, as the threshold preceded not the future but the past. The bridge as structure and thing is celebrated, in a most exclamatory poem, as "Vision of the Voyage." But the act of vision, percept as perspect, or the bringing of vision to legibility, is revealed throughout as an act of reading/interpreting and projecting an earlier text. Yet, the reading is not determined by the earlier idea or its representation. Thus Columbus's journals of his voyage or even Whitman's exhausted account of manifest destiny in "Passage to India," which are some of the matter of Crane's poem and America's textuality—that is, all these figures of the voyage as return—turn out to be little more than attempts to understand the conditions of voyaging or transport itself. The central problematic of the poem, in short, is the poem—language, metaphor, bridging, transport. The attempt in all such narratives to celebrate at once the means of transportation and to occlude it, to herald the possibility of unmediated vision, turns upon itself to re-mark the problematics of the voyage. As in Whitman's poem the points of connection are all, as it were, man-made (the Suez Canal, the transatlantic cable, the transcontinental railroad, crossing discontinuities like oceans and landmasses from East to West to confirm the "continuity of American poetry"), Crane's poem features the deferral points and the problematic media of transport. Within the poem itself, these points are its own metaphors.

Trying to induce an American dream or vision, the poet is consumed by it. He is disfigured by his own figurations, just as Columbus was, or Poe; or decapitated, like Isadora Duncan, like the figure of Poe the poet envisions in "The Tunnel" section. The poem signifies this in its modes of transportation, moving from the sailing ship of Columbus, endangered by the sea which "tests the word," to the modern conveyances whose speed and dynamics mark the vitality and entropy of the present, both signifying the capitalist ravishment forewarned in the "Ave Maria" section. Consumption and self-consumption, then, are the economic themes extended to language, themes that characterize the risk of the poet who must be sacrificed to his vision, in that he is the medium through whom the vision is to be delivered. He himself, the pariah, is the language, to echo H.D.

The Bridge is a quest poem, then, and a part of the American sublime, but it is a quest undone by the conditions of the modern sublime. That is, at every step or point, the poet finds himself marginalized or exiled in his own language, when he is forced to recognize the incommensurability of his language to his dream and can only present, as Lyotard defines the modern, "the fact that the unpresentable exists" (*Postmodern Condition*, 78). He can only reflect on his own technical expertise. The sublime "takes place," writes Lyotard, "when the imagination fails to present an object which might, if only in principle, come to match a concept." Crane's poet can only present his own heroic failure, as a repetition of an historical succession of failures. But the failure of the return, of language's stubborn incommensurability, can itself be turned, in an uncanny way, into an affirmation of the future present enacted in the poet's own performance.

Thus Crane must reject enabling myths such as the return, or such quest motifs as those Eliot appropriates from mythology and Pound from literature, or any nostalgic turn toward powerful ancestors that are both sustaining (say, Tiresius) or threatening, and live out the anxiety of influence as an influence of the future. For what lies in the future, on the horizon, is always the cryptic word. It has replaced all origins, and it both beckons and threatens. It is at once his other and his fate, his destiny. It marks his ultimate and present disfiguration, this divided word. It is like the "flashing scene" or non-origin that draws the crowd in the "Proem" toward the movie, and compels the suicide to leap from the Bridge, or sends its dynamic energy (its sunlight) "down Wall, from girder into street" (3–4). This future-present word is no longer the singularity of the *logos*, or of the symbol; and even the synecdochic bridge can only serve as emblem, holding the poet in its shadow and compelling him into new language games in order to catch its dangerous vibrancy.

The emblem, however, shares one thing with the ancient's conscious symbol, as Hegel would have it. It is a kind of Sphinx whose riddle is not exactly to be interpreted or divined in a manner which would reflect man to himself. Rather it compels a dynamics of reading. It is dynamics, the unrepresentable, itself, the ever-changing word. The bridge emblematizes history (and America) in its figuration and asks the poet not to solve its riddle but repeatedly to tell a story about it. That is the fate and destiny of all American writers. "What cunning neighbors history has in fine!" Crane exclaims in the "Quaker Hill" section (46), where he contemplates the former sacred space of the word now converted into a commercial hotel. This space is under "lease," is mortgaged, its antique "seal" materialized. It is no longer a home or meeting place (canny) but an uncanny place of dalliance and distraction. The artist's burden is always to restore its signification: "Shoulder the curse of sundered parentage" (47). But he soon discovers that it was not a seal hiding the secrets of some immanent and now lost plenitude, but the sign of a genealogical fracture that preceded origins. It was always already sundered, and the poet's heritage is derived from mortgaged texts. Every sign of the past reveals this genealogical fracture, and that America is not simply a quotation, but a quotation of a quotation. Every new poem, then, is something more than a repetition of the past. It is also, necessarily a

quotation of the act or performance of turning away; it is a troping.

Unlike Spengler's Faustian artist, who manifests his lust for
the infinite in his commitment to perspectivism, Crane finds
perspective blinding: "Perspective never withers from their
eyes," he writes of those who occupy the unheimlich space of
the "New Avalon Hotel." They are blind to the sublime as they
are to their own desires. Only the artist contemplates the
infinite, but in an ironic mode of its impossibility. Isadora Duncan's utterance serves as epigraph to "Quaker Hill," renounc-
ing the infinite in terms more applicable to Stevens's claim that
the truest belief is to believe in a fiction which is known not to
be true: "I see only the ideal. But no ideals have ever been fully
successful on this earth" (45). That would include the sublime
figure the artist makes, his or her performance, and conscious
symbols.

Every manifest form of the ideal, then, every symbol bears the
mark of artifice, reveals a *techne*. None is "fully successful." The
symbol bears within itself at once the hint of a lost natural plenitude and an indication that even nature or phenomena is only
a mechanical representation. The incompatibility of the natural and the artificial in every symbolic performance paralyzes
the poet, since he must read its double character. He cannot
make the other reflect him; nor can he possess an other's representation. The burden he "shoulder[s]" is not the history of
the past, but of producing a history, a genetic poem that will
unfold some representation of the future.

The Bridge is above all a made poem, not a visionary revelation. It dramatizes vision as a perspectival (in the Nietzschean
sense) scene of reading or interpretation in which the reader
finds himself as it were transfixed in the gaze of the symbol he is
producing. For in reading the figure in translating it, or translating its translative power, he is undone and exiled. The
bridge/symbol is a perspectival focus or concentration that
defines the crowd as it defines the abyss. And the anonymous
pariah cannot find anything but his anonymity in its turning.
The bridge has become the active agent or subject, holding the
poet in thrall. The "crowd" hastening toward the "cinema"

negates both the space of Plato's cave and Hegel's pit of memory; and the bridge, which should organize space, opens it to the accidents of history's indirection. The bridge, then, as both "harp and altar, of the fury fused" and "Terrific threshold of the prophet's pledge" (3–4), reflects only the poet's exile in his language. If it is an "unfractioned idiom, immaculate sigh of stars," it is an oxymoron. It is that which should signify at once the unity of city, country, and world history; but instead it signifies to the poet not only his double exile, but his inability to command its perspective as well. It signifies to him the condition of all historical restlessness, what Nietzsche called, in referring to the modern situation of being beyond metaphysics or the Platonic-Hegelian nostalgia, being homeless: "The City's fiery parcels all undone, / Already snow submerges an iron year."

What is given the poet as his language and his future, the bridge which he calls "threshold of the prophet's pledge," he asks to "lend a myth to God." But like every capitalist obligation, that which lends exacts some interest. The poem opens into a strange economy. To ask the symbol to "lend a myth" is to apostrophize, and to appeal to one's language to produce. It is to apostrophize the medium. And that is where the poem concludes, in an attempt to reify the genetic figure as center, noun as verb: a "Choir, translating time / Into what multitudinous Verb the sun / and synergy of waters ever fuse, recast / In myriad syllables" (56–57). Here the bridge as symbolpoem is also invoked as "index" and as "one arc synoptic of all tides below." But the "pervasive Paradigm" everywhere redoubles itself as "myriad syllables" in a kind of uncanny dissemination. "Synergy" proves to be the key and the problem, for Crane treats the bridge as a conscious symbol, virtually a modern pyramid and hieroglyph, and at the same time as a trope, subject to its temporal and historical destiny, or better, the non-destiny of entropy.

The concluding "Atlantis" section (55–58) no more resolves the problem than the introductory "Proem" managed to reify the "curveship." If the bridge is "synoptic" and an "index," it is no less a limit, and it is the marking of this limit, as both a threat and a force, that occupies the history inscribed in the poem between "Ave Maria" and "The Tunnel." If America is both *word* and *bridge*, she is also a threshold to her own self-consumption. Of "sundered parentage," and without a past, she shoulders the destiny of Hegel's future which will be a different and presently inconceivable form. Crane's sublime lies in his effort to conceive this inconceivable, to represent the unpresentable, as a kind of auto-insemination. From the beginning of the "Ave Maria" (5–8), which is a restaging of the section of Columbus's journal dealing with his anxiety over delivering back the word of his discovery, Crane's theme is not the immanent nature of a virgin land, but the risk and limit of any representation of such a "plenitude." He cannot preserve the "immaculate sigh" of the word that at every turn reveals its divided face, but as well its self-consuming force.

Crane retells Columbus's account as a moment of disfiguration and exploitation that forces the visionary to revise his own mode of revelation. That is, his own language is put at risk. Crane emphasizes the true danger of quest as the danger of the return, and thus the danger to the word (along with the quester who embodies it). Like Williams, he treats the discovery as an act of mis-naming—Columbus thinks he has found "The Chan's great continent," or Cathay—but his essential concern is with possibly failing to communicate that discovery. So he places a written record of his discovery in a cask (Crane mistakenly writes "casque," or Spanish military headgear) and sets it afloat on the stormy ocean: "For here between two worlds, another harsh, / This third, of water, tests the word." The word is always between, and at risk, because it is an "incognizable Word / Of Eden and the enchained sepulchre," thus a "parable of man" and a prayer. Crane finds Columbus's Logos, his Christian vision, already inscribed in the mast of his ship, the figure of the cross. For ship as well as "casque" bears the word and is tested. The ship as well as its captain is the word as metaphor, not the "incognizable Word."

Each section of *The Bridge* renews and repeats this questioning of the word as the media of communication, of that which is always already between. Whether bridge or ship, whether "macadam" highway stretching from "Far Rockaway to Golden Gate" in the "Van Winkle" section or the subway of "The Tunnel," Crane's figure of the poet/quester as word incarnate is always a double of the bridge/figure that consumes him in the "Proem" and "Atlantis." But a strange, disfigured double, a double with a difference. Whereas sailing ship, highway, and river signify a continuity of nature or a natural bridge, the continent is also marked by another kind of communications system and thus another kind of history—one might say a telecommunications system: the "telegraphic night" of "The River" which marks the age of "iron dealt cleavage"; or the vortex carved out by the Falcon Ace's crashing plane in "Cape Hatteras" that ends in "dispersion" and "debris." The latter both binds the modern poet hand-in-hand with Walt Whitman and cleaves them, like the difference between a natural and a dynamic language, the language of "tribal morn" ("The Dance") and "Open Road" ("Cape Hatteras") with and against the language of the "arrant page" ("Quaker Hill") or the "Refractions of the thousand theaters, faces" that connect "Times Square to Columbus Circle" in the performative and decapitating speed of "The Tunnel."

Indeed, one can read *The Bridge* as a record of this denaturalization of the word, as in the movement from "Maquokeeta's" dance to that of the stripper grinding out dull repetitions to jazz in "National Winter Garden." That is, one can read it as a repetition of the decline of the West within America's attenuated history, or within the genealogy of the American visionary poet from "Columbus" and Whitman to the modern. Yet, as we have seen, Whitman recognized his own situation as modern; and Crane's poem dramatizes Whitman's situation as caught "between two worlds" as surely as is Columbus's word. It is not, then, as if the natural threshold of Cape Hatteras is suddenly victimized and displaced by the dynamic one signified by the Wright brothers' craft. The two have always already been entangled the one in the other, not as antithetical notions of reality but as two interpretations of history. As in Henry Adams's "history," they mark an originary discontinuity that did not simply occur in the middle of the nineteenth century, falling nicely between tradition and modernity; Whitman's poetry, as Crane celebrates it in "Cape Hatteras," already inscribes the Virgin and the Dynamo, "*Paris Angelicas*" and "Falcon Ace." They mark a discontinuity as indelibly as the "barely perceptible fissure" in Usher's "House," a legacy left for each poet to "shoulder."

In contemplating his own inheritance, therefore, the modern must rely as inevitably as Columbus and Whitman upon an old idiom to name the new. Crane resisted the pessimism of Spengler's and Eliot's crisis of the modern, and sought in the violence, speed, and unrepresentable nature of modern energy, in thermodynamics and telecommunications, a kind of synergy or unity of heterogeneity and dispersal. But his task remained as impossible as was Poe's in *Eureka* or "Usher," to cover over or bridge the abyss that had opened up beneath equivocal alternatives. The old names would work only as catechreses, marking their own artifice or technical appropriation. They would have to be made into conscious symbols, but in a new and different sense. And they would not be readable except as some kind of future anterior, to borrow Lyotard's notion.

Translating Whitman's "prophetic script" into "Sanskrit charge," then, Crane re-marks figural language in spatial terms that undo the dream of closed space. He produces "abysmal cupolas of space" ("Cape Hatteras") and a new notion of history. But by embracing the dynamic within the natural, by finding the natural sublated in the dynamic, Crane gives himself up as modern poet/poem/word to the disfigurement and displacement of Poe ("The Tunnel") or the marginality of Duncan, Dickinson, and Melville in a capitalist culture. He pulls the "Umbilical" of the modern poet's genealogy and memory and writes a new history of the word without destiny or destination, repeating Whitman's call for the modern democratic poem that is still to be written and posted. He returns vision to the graphic non-representation of its own failure of representation, and thus as de Man would say, to the extreme conditions of Hegel's sublime. He submits future poetry to the fate of a dynamic entropy that will not sustain the individual self or finite consciousness—to "One Song, one Bridge of Fire" that is heterogeneous and "Whispers antiphonal in azure swing" (58). The figure on the horizon turns slowly in the wind, but it is not an aeolian harp or romantic symbol (or self) any longer. It is a bridge of another kind and without a proper name.

Chapter Four
Stein and Bergson

It has always seemed to me a rare privilege, this, of being an American, a real American, one whose tradition it has taken scarcely sixty years to create. We need only realise our parents, remember our grandparents and know ourselves and our history is complete. (Stein, *The Making of Americans*)[1]

I

Gertrude Stein knew that the writing of an American genealogy involved a repetition and undoing of the idea of genealogy itself, just as the "making of Americans" and the invention of "American" writing (say, a "great American novel") would involve a generic intervention, a kind of genre-cide. Recall the notable opening of *The Making of Americans*, which inscribes the genealogical resistance to all newness, including any new writing: "Once an angry man dragged his father along the ground through his own orchard. 'Stop!' cried the groaning old man at last, 'Stop!' I did not drag my father beyond this tree" (MA, 3). Writing, she knew, was a kind of dragging along of the past and inherited conventions, yet a return upon old ground. But it must also be a refurrowing of that ground and a displacement of the father—not a mixing of "memory and desire" (Eliot) but a beginning again of remembering. Writing would always be some kind of future anterior, performative rather than descriptive or memorial. "America" for her was another name for this disturbing *act* of writing, this writing writing itself.

"America," for Stein, has no referent as such, just as America has no history, no true identity. "America" is modernity and its identity is futural, deferred. *It* will have *to be* written. This seems to be the problematic at issue in *The Geographical History of America* where she makes clear that the question of writing and the question of identity are interrelated: "What is a sentence for if I am I then my little dog knows me." That phrase in *How to Write* (19) becomes the refrain around which she develops the "play" of writing. For Stein, writing, and not saying, is originary, and she marks the double grammar of the act ("What is a sentence for if I am I . . ." "What is a sentence for? If I am I . . ."). Writing produces a "human nature," she continues, not a "human mind," a nature or other to which the unreflective little dog responds, a naturalness of identity before and beyond reflection. Writing is not self-reflective. It knows no negative, no "No": "The human mind has no resemblances if it had it could not write that is to say write right" (GHA, 99). In writing, the "human mind" might find its anterior in "human nature," overcoming or effacing the dualisms that have haunted western humanism in the form of thinking oneself.

Writing is act, performative, play, repetition: "the human mind can write and so cannot any dog and so human writing is not human nature but human mind" (GHA, 77); "No human nature does not play. . . . A dog plays because he plays again" (GHA, 100). But the human mind can make plays, plays which display that mind as writing performance, thus mimicking human nature (see GHA, 99–100). Plays manifest mind and memory, as Bergson might say; or better, they materialize a simulacrum of memory not as some past, determining trace and trait, but as an active and present movement. Human nature cannot write, but can only be written (GHA, 105). To write the geo-graphic history of America is to manifest America as an originary force, an autogenetic force, a repetition in/as writing. Writing is beginning again. America, "America," is not the end of history, the period to the sentence of the West and another *Bridge* or "Passage to India," a repetition or eternal return of the same. It is, to the contrary, a strange repetition, a beginning again of the human mind. This mind is not an identity, then. It is not substantive or a *cogito* but an energy that incessantly displaces itself, like writing: "The human mind has not begun it happens once in a while but it has not begun" (GHP, 178). What it originates, by repetition, is itself, but it is not an *it* (*id*). It is not a fallen unity desiring its full identity, but always already a heterogeneity. Thus, all American writing will be against the sentence, and its closure, as well as against the totality, the "flatness," as she calls it, of "masterpieces." The originary repetition of American writing is autobiographical self-production.

Autobiography, like geographical history, then, does not have the structure of an I reflecting itself, essentializing itself as the unity of mind and nature. Stein rejects philosophy precisely because of its reflexive grammar, its commitment to the sentence and to the narrative circle: "But when you are one you are through with philosophy, because philosophy has to talk to itself about it" (GHA, 186), that is, reflect on itself as essential I. Writing has always already begun, and autobiography as writing-repetition produces a new sense of I as time, as already begun and beginning again, rather than reflecting a life or "bios." It produces "time," but time, as we will see, as the name of the genetic or originary, time as uncanny duration, one might say. This is not quite, however, the subjective time of the Romantics, or the "human time" of phenomonology, and though we will have occasion to draw some parallels between Stein's writing and Bergson's *durée*, as against say, Hegel's "finite consciousness," Stein's time will have to be examined on a model of language Bergson rejects. She begins with an I who writes, but is in turn written, an I who is many and whose identity is already distributed through the words it maneuvers, separates, and rejoins:

In the first place think of words apart or together. It makes everybody happy to have words together. It makes everybody happy to have words apart. Either may not have anything whatsoever to do with human nature.

Any word may and does not have anything whatever to do with identity too.

Nor with time.

There are no tears when you say and not with time.

Not either when you say not with identity.

It carefully comes about that there is no identity and no time and

therefore no human nature when words are apart.
Or rather when words are together. (GHA, 204–5)

"Identity is very curious," she continues, and can no longer be thought on the model of self-reflexivity: "I am I because my little dog knows me," and "when he does not know me am I I" (GHA, 205, 206—note the omission of a question mark). Words written are addressed "to somebody" (except, as she says, in the case of masterpieces which seem to be for themselves, totalized works), and thus addressed to an other which is necessary to confirm the sender's identity. Identity is always double, at least, and heterogeneous: "Anything that can be lost is something anybody can get used to and that is identity" (GHA, 207). Identity is at once confirmed and lost, just as the dog's knowing depends not on its reception of a meaning but its recognition of the love of address that relates and separates mind and nature. Even human identity depends on the possibility of loss: "At a distance we say a man on a bicycle and at a distance he looked like two"; "And so identity is not a ball, no not at all" (GHA, 209).

Identity, however, if not a ball, is figurally manifest, as in writing, the address that separates self and other. Thus she defines poetry as something seen, though by this she does not mean simple perception nor a record of understanding, an intentionality: "Poetry may be time but if it is then it is remembered time and that makes it be what is seen" (GHA, 210). This poetry is different from a masterpiece because what is seen is repeatedly seen, re-seen in a scene, and is thus a kind of insight, an intertextual overlay of past-present rememberings and present sensings. The past, then, comes as if from the future, in old words disengaged from the patina of etymological sense, words that appear in their new relations like paleonyms or vestiges of meanings to be. Stein locates memory not in some mental act of recall but in writing—for example, the detective story, which she celebrates as an American genre, that treats remembering as the tracking of clues, a recall of the absent dead: "About detective stories is the trouble with them that the one that is dead has no time and no identity for him to them and yet they think that they can remember what they do not have as having it without their having it for them" (GHA, 213–14). This kind of writing deconstructs the old grammar of identity, the sentence whose closure is ordered by the grammatical subject. Reading a detective story, she suggests, leads one to repeat this construction of identity, this writing. Detective stories, then, are not a hermeneutic, a recuperation of some lost truth or past crime, but a repetition of the play of identity. It is a repetition, as she indicates in a passage remarking on the question of Hamlet, of the displacement of the subject-father, by the son who cannot himself be father or even catch in his own play the conscience or essence of the King. Thus *Hamlet* the play is transcribed into a detective story, an allegory of writing that, she writes, cannot be "led" in a direct line but is like a "figure" which "wanders on alone" (GHA, 241). (We will return in the last section of this essay to what "leads" in writing: not the grammatical subject but the "wrist.") The "little dog" that "knows me" leads in this instance, since it does not conceive or reflect one's identity as the "human mind" may do. It leads one to rethink oneself, to rethink the self as relation: "The person and the dog are there and the dog is there and the person is there and where oh where is their identity is the identity there anywhere. / Every century is not every century nor every country not every country has what they know is not identity" (GHA, 242–43). A living person's and a living nation's identity are never achieved, but always deferred, like this text of repetitive sentences which ends, "I am not sure that is not the end" (GHA, 243).

II

Like most of Stein's (and perhaps all "American") texts, *Geographical History* is an autobiography, an allegory of her and America's writing her (it) self. It is phrased in the language of genealogy yet it suspends the diagrammatic logic of genealogy. Like so many American writers of her time, Stein was preoccupied with the changing senses of time and history that brought the old master narratives of tradition into question, for example, the great metanarratives of universal or monumental history (Hegel, say), the grand works of European literature, the family romances. Yet, as she understood, this undoing and rewriting of the old grammar, this effort to "make it new," would in a sense repeat and parody the old metanarratives and might even appear, like the late novels of Henry James, to be consummate formal masterpieces. But they are really something else, different or separate types of writing: self-reflexive fictions containing interpretative scenes undoing the center, commentaries that revise, re-see, and rewrite themselves, as Henry James would say in one of his prefaces, into the "story of my story." The preface becomes autobiography and the autobiography a prefacing anteriority to the new. These stories of time-to-be would have to take into account their own supplemental writing, and a certain randomness and irreversibility. However much they might seem to be masterpieces at a later time, they would expose something irregular in the hand that wrote (led) them.

One might even read Stein's iconic modern poem, "a rose is a rose . . ." written in a circle, as such a story or grammatical revision. For Stein, this is the figure of writing that every story tells about itself. To repeat: "A sentence has wishes as an event"; "What is a sentence for if I am I then my little dog knows me" (HW, 18, 19). "A sentence is not emotional a paragraph is," she repeats several times in different contexts, in repetitions that resist the sentence's closure, its logical and reflexive return to the subject-father. For Stein, writing (Stein's writing) paragraphs, undoing the sentence, introducing into the circle of the return an excess:

> Now for a sentence. Welcome to hurry. That is either a sentence or a part of a sentence if it is a part of a sentence the sentence is he is welcome to hurry. Welcome is in itself a part of a sentence. . . .
> Welcome when they come. Are they welcome when they come.
> A sentence instead of increases. It should be if they are. Welcome when they come. That so easily makes a paragraph. Try again.
> They made made them when they were by them. This is a sentence. It has no use in itself because made is said two times. (HW, 26)

Writing not only reveals the redundancy of language—it exploits it, explicates it. It exposes the grammatological model, and reveals what modern information theory tries to explain, the entropy that undoes all such models. Stein's examination of "Arthur A Grammar" (a chapter in *How to Write*) explores this inescapable excess or "increase" that makes it impossible for any new writing to return to the mastery of the author ("Arthur is an author," 58) and the time of the sentence ("Grammar. One two three completely," 71). As we will see later, this old grammar already inscribes the new (as "increase"), which Stein will describe as *one plus one plus one* to infinity. The old grammar and the old word always already bear another futural sense: "To-morrow is grammar. . . . To study a desire to continue" (HW, 81). Writing is repetition with a difference ("Try it again happen. / Trying it again happen. / What is the difference between came and went," 83). It doubles grammar and increases the sentence ("Grammar may may be to withdrew. / Grammar may not be likeness," 84). Thus, "Archie a grammar" (HW, 87), subject-author (archē), is displaced by a different and plural generic force: "Winifred a grammar," "Susan a grammar," and "Germaine and grammar," among other phrases for this disseminative force. What is germane to grammar becomes its new signature, and the new time-space it organizes, like the ordinary house of ordinary objects, food, and rooms in *Tender Buttons*, to which we will return in the last section. The old space of things, their given relation as understanding, or the time they apparently mark as orderly succession, is doubled back upon itself, not in a self-reflexive grammar, but as a double exposure: "There may be in grammar two sentences that commence as one" (HW, 96). Identity is a simultaneity as difference, and grammar is originarily "mistaken" (HW, 84).

Grammar, she concludes, bears within itself not simply an other and opposing force, but an originary disturbance. As if reflecting on her *Tender Buttons*, she writes that the truth of new grammar is "that it is tender" (HW, 97), that is, clitoral rather than phallic, not an absence of phallogocentric presence but a different kind of doubling force (of this, much later). It exposes the old grammar's authority, that it is "contained in the father," and reveals why men have grown "thinner and thinner and old men thinner" until we can now recognize that the subject resides in the "daughter(s)" (HW, 99). It turns the sentence toward (into) the paragraph, the logical father (constative) into its emotional and intuitive undoing (rhetorical, performative). More than once, Stein offers an historical analogy for her view of this transformation of models: sentences characterize the eighteenth century, the Enlightenment; the nineteenth century or romantic thought appears in the phrase or fragment; and the twentieth century's mark is the paragraph, the continuum. But the latter, while a continuum or repetition without beginning or ending, is heterogeneous rather than homogeneous, multiple rather than singular, equivocal rather than univocal, and thus not continuous in any determinate sense. They reveal the sentence to be self-transformative rather than self-reflexive or closed. Paragraphs are feminine rather than masculine, but the first is not simply a displacement of the second, since it inscribes within its turnings all the elements of what it displaces. It degenders or marginalizes gender difference.

Paragraphs, then, signify a future anterior time, what Stein calls in her most famous formulation a "continuous present" rather than a "prolonged present" (the past extended through present toward future, or what Heidegger called the "vulgar sense" of time) of traditional narrativity, a distinction she makes in the often misread essay, "Composition as Explanation." A "continuous present" would not be a simple present, the unity of the here and now, as in the metaphysical notion of time (either Kant's or Hegel's, say), but is a time conditioned and even strangely determined by the future. It is a heterogeneous present-not-now. Paragraphs, in Stein's compositional lexicon, transact a new sense of time, for paragraphs are without beginning and end, without period, and therefore compose what we might call a dys-lexic continuum. "America," like the modern century, is one name for this not yet present, "modernity" yet another. We will return to this future later.

III

According to Nietzsche, the idea of man as subject, as thinker or doer, depends on the precondition of belief, "our belief in the 'ego' as a substance": "But that a belief, however necessary it may be for the preservation of a species, has nothing to do with truth, one knows for the fact that, e.g., we have to believe in time, space, and motion, without feeling compelled to grant them absolute reality."[2] The concept of time is therefore a metaphysical postulate that is tied to our belief in the subject, the will as substance. And yet it is only a belief to which we cannot grant the status of truth. The psychological notion of the ego as thinker-doer resides in the metaphysical postulate of the subject as the origin and determinant of time, yet a subject that unfolds as and in time, overcoming itself. This subject is a changing substance and thus not a substance at all. Nietzsche's reformulation of the notion of the subject not only suspends Hegel's erection of the grammatical subject but anticipates the conditions of Freud's pleasure-pain principle and thus the psychoanalytical breakdown of the unified, substantive self.

No subsequent conceptualization of time has been able to go beyond or resolve the *aporia* of this self-opposition. Nor has any literary manifestation, expression, or representation of something like subjective or human time been able to reconstruct a viable phenomenological subject. The attempt, for example, to formulate critically the modes of human time in the psychological or stream-of-consciousness novel, or of life in such quasi-genre as autobiography, or even the time-of-act of the mind in Romantic and post-Romantic poetry, always brings us back to this question of time's metaphysical texture. There is no such thing as a "vulgar concept of time," writes Jacques Derrida in regard to Heidegger's argument in *Being and Time* that he was prepared to think beyond metaphysics and its formulation of time as circular, repeatable, and therefore ontotheological. In his "*Ousia* and *Gramme*: Note on a Note from *Being and Time*" (in *Margins*, 31–67), Derrida submits Heideggerean "woodnotes" to a deconstructive reading that indicates why the modern philosopher is bound to repeat the very gesture that he condemns metaphysics for making, from Aristotle through Hegel to Bergson. Each of which, according to Heidegger and Derrida, locates the concept of time upon the "point" of the present, interpreting time as space, despite even such arguments as Bergson's against this spatialization. The task of Derrida's reading, his note on a note, serves not only to disrupt and reveal the musical analogy by which certain thinkers hope to undo the spatial representation of time, but argues in effect for the impossibility of thinking beyond metaphysics. Time can only be thought in terms of Being, and being present.

All this, in sum, in order to suggest:

1. That perhaps there is no "vulgar concept of time." The concept of time, in all its aspects, belongs to metaphysics, and it names the domination of presence. Therefore we can only conclude that the entire system of metaphysical concepts, throughout its history, develops the so-called "vulgarity" of the concept of time . . . , but also that an *other* concept of time cannot be opposed to it, since time in general belongs to metaphysical conceptuality. In attempting to produce this *other* concept, one rapidly would come to see that it is constructed out of other metaphysical or ontotheological predicates. (63)

A new time would appear in the vestiges of old words, paleonyms, like a conceptual hybrid. It would be a kind of reading of time, or a double writing. In the process of explaining Heidegger's effort to position himself beyond metaphysics and, especially, Bergson's position (Heidegger emphasizes Bergson's rejection of quantitative or spatial temporality, but still finds in the concept of *durée* or qualitative, subjective time, a residually vulgar ground in the presence of self), Derrida marks the limits of all such thinking beyond metaphysics, its appeal "to a less narrow determination of presence from a more narrow determination of it" (*Margins*, 65). He concludes that while Heidegger sets the metaphysical edifice of western thought—that is, thought constructed upon an untroubled concept of being—atremble, he cannot produce a distinct signature or a different text that is not already imbricated with what it rejects. Thus, where Heidegger rethinks Being as "primordial temporality," Derrida finds something "older" than being, *différance.*

Derrida's reading of *différance* and *trace,* against Heidegger's effort to locate the horizon of Being as existential *Fallen,* does not reject Heidegger's reading of Bergson, but reveals why Heidegger must repeat the blindness he exposes in the Bergsonian "trace." He thereby shows why every effort to "make it new" is a problem of writing, an effort to produce a "writing without presence and without absence, without history, without cause, without *archia*, without *telos*, a writing that absolutely upsets all dialectics, all theology, all teleology, all ontology" (*Margins*, 67). We might also add, for the writer of literature it would demand a writing beyond literature, a displacement of the old genealogical order and the narrative cycle, the "house of fiction."

For Derrida, of course, there is no manifest example of this different *writing*, except as it appears in old traces (and the same holds for the word *trait* as for writing). Thus, even the example of experimental writing or abstract art cannot serve to mark a modernist or postmodernist break with tradition, just as Derrida's own double-writing remains inscribed within the conventions of philosophical discourse. The new, then, bears traces of the old, but these are traces of traces, just as familiarities of tradition echo within the dissonances and parodic graphematics of experiment and improvisation. To attempt to write a new philosophy or to write beyond philosophy, whether like Bergson or Heidegger, condemns one to a limit that inevitably, according to Derrida, turns up like a signature in the new work. Thus Gertrude Stein's modernist break, that is, the appearance of the critical act within her creative distortions, her marginalizing of the literary masterpiece.

Stein was present in Paris at the time when Bergsonian thought was at the height of fashion and influence, especially as a provocation to some of the experiments of what became literary modernism. And she lived well beyond the decline of Bergson's impact, both as philosopher and aesthetic provocateur, evident in such reactions as Eliot's early enthusiasm for and moral revulsion against the philosopher's subjectivism or T. E. Hulme's qualified embrace of and orthodox resistance to the modern romantic. And she knew well the theoretical orthodoxy of reaction manifest so polemically in Wyndham Lewis's *Time and Western Man* which denounced almost all experiment—Stein's, Joyce's (with some qualification), Pound's, even Chaplin's modern times—as the logical (or illogical) issue of a romanticism that developed from Rousseau to Bergson and that had infiltrated science in the form of "Einsteinian flux": "The philosophy of the space-timers is identical with the old, and as many people had hoped, exploded Bergsonian philosophy of psychological time (or *durée*, as he called it)."[3] According to Lewis, Stein's writing was an "attack upon the logical architecture of words," and Pound's is "lost halfway between one art and another" (*Time*, 114).

Though Lewis's obsession with the decadence of the *spacetimers* of modernism is only one version of the contradictions out of which twentieth-century literary experiment developed, in itself it is a remarkable icon of our skewed literary history. That history postures as a philosophical analysis of modern thought's retreat into irrationality, what Hulme called the "spilt religion" of a romantic century, and it marks distinctly the wrestle Eliot had with the questions of truth, self, and words. In other words, Lewis's argument for the imperatives of objective thought is nothing more than a testy moralistic defense of *Logos* theology in which a certain (and nostalgic) tradition of classicism is reclaimed as the secular survival of religious fragmentation. This attempt to maintain the religious within the secular marks the struggle of modernism, in literature and philosophy, to maintain some kind of "panlogism" (Jacques Maritain's term, applied to Hegel) apart from religious orthodoxy and within the individual self's mastery of the word. Bergson's philosophy of "spontaneous action" or intuition, according to Maritain, represents the logical consequences of Hegelianism, for it signifies the danger of submitting to the lure of becoming an "uninterrupted change," from which the univocal word will never be regathered and the finite consciousness will become increasingly fragmented and isolated, losing contact with its organizing center, the intellect.

Bergson, then, becomes one of those metonymic figures for the amoral decision modernism evidenced when it turned away from the word to the *Abgrund* of pure subjectivism, making an attack, like Stein's, on "the logical architecture of words." For the self as *archē* was itself always already the fragmented *logos*. And Bergson's attempt to account for the univocality of the multiple seemed to critics like Lewis and Maritain the predicative sign of modern despair, the death of philosophical history at the hand of a disseminative writing. But that death leaves behind a certain sense of time, that which remains inscribed in metaphysics. Though, as Lewis indicates, Bergson's reign at the center of philosophy in the early twentieth century was short-lived, his preoccupation with a new thought of time would continue as a kind of template in the developments of literary modernism.

Hence Lewis's attack on the "psychologism" of the space-timers and his advocacy of a return to a certain classical impersonalism, his argument for the work of art as univocal, homogeneous object as against Bergson's "virtual" yet heterogeneous interiority. The threat of Nietzsche's questioning of the subject or, what might seem but was not its opposite, Bergson's essentializing of an ever-changing, heterogeneous consciousness, was both a lure and a danger to modernism, in Lewis's and Eliot's notion, and led to their reaction against it, even as it provoked Pound and others to a different sense of what making it new might involve—let us call it the deconstruction and translation of tradition.[4] For Bergsonism made clear what Eliot had already gleaned from Hegelian and post-Hegelian phenomenologies of mind-spirit, the insubstantiality of the self, its transitory fate. Bergsonian rewriting of the self as intuition, while intended to free the individual from past determinations, resubjected the self to Hegelian negation. For it allowed the self ceaselessly to re-write itself, re-draft itself, in a movement without direction, or *telos*. The writers of modernism—those who were writing the modern, one might say—like Pound and Stein, recognized what Nietzsche confronted, and what Bergson tried to repress: that this writing I could no longer be staged as a self-world dialectic, that it no longer was the subject of language (or logocentric) but was dispersed among the words.

IV

We might begin again with the question of time as Bergson formulated it—that time, in its classical conception (Heidegger's "vulgar sense of time"), had always been represented as space, as a succession of points or presents (nows) and thus by the metaphor of line and circle. For Bergson, despite Lewis's later contention, even Einsteinian physics did not radically alter this condition, since the fourth dimension remained quantitative and, in effect, spatial. Bergson's critique of time as spatiality consisted of an inversion or interiorizing of time, focusing on what he called the "qualitative" in contrast to the "quantitative," the former being expressible only in a new set of word-concepts—intuition, duration, matter and memory, virtuality and actuality, and so on—which some commentators like Gilles Deleuze claim are more than mere neologisms.[5] Suffice it to say that, as Heidegger and Derrida point out, these new concepts remain metaphysical in essence and are thus tied to the very conceptual system from which they were extracted and were intended to rewrite. It is the conditions of their hybridity, of determining whether they simply repeat by inversion and thus confirm the old system, or whether they make that system tremble (as Heidegger claimed for his reading of Bergson's Aristotelianism, that is, for his effort to rethink time, beyond metaphysics) that has allowed Deleuze to propose a new, poststructural Bergsonism, and allows us to rethink the effects of Bergsonian thought that are at work in literary modernisms.

We should note three things: first, Bergson's critique of Einsteinian relativism resists the equation of Bergsonism with the space-timers defined by Lewis, who saw in the Frenchman's psychologism a moral relativity theory; second, that Bergson's "theory" is not a psychological theory but an effort toward a new ontology (or phenomenology); and third, that Bergson encounters in his construction of a new metaphysics and new method (intuition, as Maritain and Deleuze point out, is a method, not a faculty) the problem of all new thought, that it must find its expression in old words and risk having its conceptual power reduced by being identified with a genealogy of thought: for example, reading Bergsonian intuition in its relation to and difference from Kant's.

"Words," Bergson wrote in *Creative Mind*, "can express the new only as a rearrangement of the old."[6] Language, therefore, is an instrument, and unrelated to Being. Thought itself, so long as it is tied to languages, is therefore discursive, abstract, inessential: a position that seriously indicts the effectiveness of all philosophical discourse, including Bergson's. Thus, when Bergson comes to celebrate literature as the most intuitive of expressions, he remains caught within a problematics that also haunted Heidegger's language of Being. In other words,

Bergson's dismissal of paleonymic abstractness, his more or less pragmatist notion of the way new concepts evolve by acting upon old, anticipates the *aporias* that poststructural discourse uncovers in all systematic (self-reflexive or dialectical) thinking, and in literature as well. For example, in his reading of Nicholas Abraham's psychoanalytic theory of discipline transference—that is, what occurs when a developing new discipline, in this case, Freudianism, borrows its word-concepts from another so-called discipline, in this case, phenomenology—Derrida underscores the question of *anasemia* or the manner in which the new words, which are also the old ones, at once move toward and away from an illusorily stable semantic and conceptual field.[7] What Bergson calls the rearrangement of old into new, Derrida marks as a "theory of errata," since the transformation of the concept—say, intuition—takes place in a margin of meanings, so that the apparently new concept is neither new nor old, neither unique nor determined, and will function tropologically or at least with certain graphematic effects in the discourse of the new discipline. The new discipline is never pure or closed. This is by way of saying that Bergson's effort to divest metaphysics, and his theory of time, of language's burden, of the *gramme* or writing, is destined (if that is the right word, and it is not) for a different reading, a reading of writing, if one might point to the developments of modernist experiment. Just as the discourses of philosophy and those of a postphilosophical "science" are hybridized, intertextual discourses, so is literary writing. Despite Bergson's appeal to art's, especially literature's, capacity for escaping language's limits, and for realizing an immediate and seamless "virtuality," what he really seems to have effected is a way of understanding the limits as a textual field, a space without boundaries, a field of effects rather than reflections and reflexes.

In any event, Bergson opened up, more for post-Hegelian aesthetics and literature than for philosophy, a somewhat different kind of phenomenology of time. And as Deleuze has revealed, it initiated a poststructural sense of temporality that offered various and contradictory formal possibilities to the linear narrative tradition. And also, to the metaphysics of voice. Bergson was as critical as Nietzsche of thought's and language's abstractness (which he associated with spatiality), but he was less ironic about the possibility of rendering (or even conceptually describing) the reality of materialized consciousness. We will return to this reinscription of the word as image later. For while Bergson's conviction, that literature was a better exemplum or even materialization of *durée* than any philosophical discourse, seems analogous to Heidegger's hypostatizing of poetic language as the "house of Being," the Bergsonian theory remains at once more traditional and more postmodern than the Heideggerean. The question is focussed, as we will see, on the idea of the image, an idea analyzed trenchantly by Deleuze in a study which begins with a reasoned explanation of why Bergson's rejection of the moving picture (as a succession of spatial figures repeating the old concept of time) was in fact the blind spot of his philosophy.[8] Deleuze argues that, to the contrary, the cinematic movement could be read as a continuation of Bergson's post-narrative theory, just as earlier, in his previously noted short and often cryptically condensed study of *Bergsonism*, Deleuze had shown just how this philosopher of interiority and prophet of modernism, who had virtually disappeared from the *mise en scène* of modern philosophy he had seemed to invent, might be recuperated within the *skepsis* of a different theory.

If *durée* is Bergson's grounding word-concept for "human time," it is neither just another (temporal) substrate for the spatial and substantive *cogito*, as in Poulet's phenomenology, nor a euphemism of Hegel's finite consciousness, that provisional (becoming) unity of the universal spirit in its alienated state. In sum, it is not another word for the psychological or singular *sum*, the "simple separate person" (Whitman). The concept, while metaphysical through and through as Heidegger argues, problematizes itself. Duration, as Deleuze forcefully revises it, implies in the name of continuity and repetition something other, difference and multiplicities, just as Gertrude Stein's "continuous present," as we will see, is neither the unity of a continuum in the classical sense nor an homogeneous and eternal now. To account for the heterogeneity of a continuum, or the possibility of the new inscribed within the old, Bergson had to account for something outside the dialectical process of oppositions. He had to account for the freedom of mind and thus for a certain *jeu* of consciousness. In contrast to Hegel, there could not properly be a Bergsonian I that says itself while at the same time altering or revising itself. Thus, qualitative interiority is always in a state of movement. It cannot have position; yet it is inseparable from its materialization. The question of "matter and memory," however, could not be thought in terms of the old inside-outside relationship, nor creativity conceived as the priority of mind, as self-creating, to matter. The language of time is responsible for this misconception, he argues, in *Creative Mind,* since it is always a language of understanding which situates the self in a "series of positions" (CM, 15).

Duration, then, is not dialectical, and not a simple interaction of past and present. The continuum of *durée* is already made up, if that is the phrase, of multiplicities, of past images which are always present (though not as presences). The unity of mind is heterogeneous, its singularity uniquely social as well as individual. Its freedom is a determined indeterminacy. For freedom and creativity are Bergson's theme, and his problem is how to account for them outside of the old genealogical formulas: how to preserve a past which is always already present, as images, yet not let it decide the present, its future? It would seem, then, a question of how to undo succession, perhaps with a notion of simultaneity. Bergsonian *durée* in effect seeks to supplant the old space-time metaphors with a reality before yet beyond metaphor, but can do so only by a revisionary return to figuration, the image. The classical or vulgar time he displaces (in which space is juxtaposition and time succession) must lead him back, as it were, to another spatio-temporal conception, the movement of past and present images into each others' fields, according to ratios (or factors) that defy quantitative calculation. If this does not escape the "vulgar sense of time," as Heidegger and Derrida point out, it does recalculate the space-time metaphor in a different sense, as a presence not present to itself, as a self without position. The line and the circle become unilinear and irreversible. The self as memory cannot remount the stream of time. Time does not move from past to present, nor can we proceed from the present into a real past. Time is not circular. Duration's virtuality may have to be defined or described in the received metaphors ("vulgar sense of time"), but then, as Bergson argues, this is simply the limitations of language, its spatiality, something that only a literary language, as we have seen, might overcome. Yet language is instrumental in advancing and refining the mind, in its creative activity. Literary writing would not only mime consciousness but would enhance it, develop or create it, and individualize it, record its materiality.

In "Introduction to Metaphysics," Bergson acknowledges his own difficulty in defining "*duration in general*":

> If I try to *analyze* duration, that is to resolve it into ready-made concepts, I am certainly obliged by the very nature of the concept and the analysis, to take two opposing views of *duration in general,* views with which I shall then claim to recompose it. This combination can present neither a diversity of degrees nor a variety of forms: it is or it is not. I shall say, for example, that there is, on the one hand, a *multiplicity* of successive states of consciousness and, on the other hand, a *unity* which binds them together. Duration will be the "synthesis" of this unity and multiplicity, but how this mysterious operation can admit of shades or degrees,—I repeat—is not quite clear. In this hypothesis there is, there can only be, a single duration, that in which our consciousness habitually operates. . . . But if, instead of claiming to analyze duration (that is, in reality, to make a synthesis of it with concepts), one first installs oneself in it by an effort of intuition, one has the feeling of a certain well-defined *tension,* whose very definiteness seems like a choice between an infinity of possible durations. This being so one perceives any number of durations, all very different from one another, even though each one of them, reduced to concepts, that is to say, considered externally from two opposite points of view, is always brought back to the indefinable combination of the multiple and the one. (CM, 184–85)

This critique of the limits of philosophical discourse could well be submitted to a close rhetorical analysis, but what is of significance for our purposes here is to note Bergson's argument that philosophy needs to go beyond or beneath philosophical language and reach intuition. He argues elsewhere that literature or literary language is both an "intuitive" miming of the rhythms of this consciousness and a production of it, but not a representation of concepts of consciousness, let alone an analysis. In doing so, he reproduces the age-old argument over the priority of poetry to philosophy, or vice versa, without however resolving anything. But it does help us to understand Bergson's effort to substitute the image for language, and why this image or collect of images (multiplicities) restricts him to a notion of writing that he otherwise seeks to efface.

In *Bergsonism*, Deleuze exploits this acknowledged contradiction in Bergson's own discourse, in a way to suggest that intuition does not in the end resolve the limits of analysis. The question of the one and the many, which as Deleuze points out was already denounced by Plato, is reinscribed by Bergson, but as a resistance to dialectics, so that what remains is a conceptual intuition of consciousness as an homogeneous heterogeneity, an oxymoron for the mind that is at once unique or individual and yet composed by a multiplicity of common and socially marked images. This mind bears no negatives, and few heirs. Its past is a present-past. Its memory is not preserved or recuperated *traits*, but present images which are constantly modified by other, experiential images. The interaction of past and present, which are no longer distinct points, in our interior life can only be defined as an incessant and indivisible movement and a simultaneity of differences, yet a unity that is marked by discontinous breaks.

As Deleuze points out, Bergson probably takes his figure of mind as a unity of multiplicities from the mathematician Georg Riemann, in order to make an argument opposing mathematics or quantification as a conceptual language.[9] Riemann was a precursor of Einstein and relativity physics, and the mathematician of transformational systems (of the interaction of differential surfaces, for example, that eventually led to Buckminster Fuller's theory of geodesic structures), whose work complements that of nineteenth-century physicists in revising concepts of change. Just as Freud appropriated the metaphors of thermodynamics (the simultaneous conservation and dissipation of energy) to articulate his pleasure/reality principle, Bergson generalized the complexity of Riemann's multiplicities into a general metaphor of duration, of the movement or process of mind that did not simply repeat itself (or the past) but could manifest itself, indeed materialize itself, in seamless and cease-less activity that nevertheless produced unique and different entities, images. Made up of interacting images, this mind pro-duced still more in creating itself, by a kind of ante-movement, and even auto-insemination. This mind was not determined but free, though the interaction of images (always present memory images inmixing with present stimuli) which at once repeat and modify each other into natural forms (and even words) develop in ways not strictly telic. These materialized forms or images in turn are interruptions of or deflections from the energy process, congealings of spirit:

> . . . this creation is a simple act of the mind, and action has only to make a pause, instead of continuing into a new creation, in order that, of itself, it may break up into words which dissociate themselves into letters which are added to all the letters which are already in the world. (CE, 253)

In this "act of the mind" (and one is quick to recall here Stevens's metaphor for modern poetry), the mind manifests it-self as congealed matter, but in another view, it is no less a force, a transitional force between differentials that ultimately goes beyond the old letters, and images, to add to or supple-ment itself and the world. Mind is virtual language, writing, which literally almost *explicates* itself. It is a multiple producing multiples, dissociated as marks or letters which do not simply add to a whole or totality. And while this congealing of mind as matter is a kind of death of thought (as abstraction or form), there is no negative as such in this spatial materialization. The mind's corpse is virtual, not complete, and open, without *telos*. Its economy is an entropic genealogy. Gertrude Stein would see that this elevation of the notion of intuition into a method would demand a new narrative line—perhaps not a narrative at all—that would parody the conventional circle by opening it to unanticipated new forms or lives, produced in new, dissociated letters adding to the old ones. She would recognize what is in-volved in the new novel moving toward novelty. "A rose is a rose . . ." as ex-centric and distortive circle becomes not only the icon of decentering modernism, but is a figure of unilinear, non-reflexive, irreversible genealogy of mind; or better, an icon of a new grammar of mind she also called American.

V

The notion of time as "continuous present" is at once the most famous and most notorious of Stein's critical concepts. For it has regularly been read as a theoretical proposition or concept defining the univocity of human time as it is presented in the individual literary character—that is, as a style of subjective representation. Whatever the concept may owe to Bergson—and one should quickly renounce any claim of the influence of philosophy upon literary construction in this instance—the "continuous present" offers us a number of (problematical) keys to Stein, a number of keys to her problematics. In other words, as always, it is not at all a concept, or even a useful descriptive term for criticism, but is itself a critical intervention, a self-interfering word-concept. As critical description, it seems to name a composed moment, a stylistic rendering or miming of a virtual time, in which reality is made or materialized by repetition. Yet, in Stein's definition, it is a proposition of deferral: "Composition is not there, it is *going to be* there and we are here" (SW, 516–17). Composition is time produced as space, it would appear, except that Stein denies it position ("there") and emphasizes it as a futural virtuality ("going to be"), and thus that which is never finally composed. Composition is explicating, unfolding, not a simultaneity of differences in relation, but supplementary repetition. It is performative rather than cognitive.

Stein does not claim that literature, as distinguished from critical or philosophical discourse, either captures or represents some reality or past, like a memory machine. She indicates that this reality of composition is not simply a mediation or becoming, but something engendered. It is a genetic act itself—uncannily, both inaugural and repetitional. Here she seems to join not only Bergson but the entire Aristotelian tradition in making time productive or genetic. But this is not quite what she claims. Composition is also explanation, that is, a kind of resistance to any unbroken or univocal sense of time as energy stream. In moving something, itself, from here to there, composition explains, explains itself, composes, and reveals its own artifices. "Continuous present," then, is both an oxymoron and a tautology, continuously implying at once succession and unity, difference and univocality. Stein, however, in a paragraph that doubly marks her coinage, attempts to distinguish between her "continuous present" and what she calls the "prolonged present," and then proceeds to say that her two most indelible critical phrases, "continuous present" and "beginning again and again," "are not the same": "Continuous present is one thing and beginning again and again is another thing. There are both things. And then there is using everything" (SW, 518). And what, one asks in quotation—"what is a thing?"

Before Heidegger, this would be the question for modernism, for the writer's desire to produce or invent rather than reflect or represent reality. One cannot read Stein's criticism as either criticism or literary theory, nor her meditation on narrative time as indifferent to this problem of how to make it new, since its own repetition is a parodic narrative of the time of explanation. To put it another way, Stein opens up for us what Derrida finds in all of the metaphysics of time, from Aristotle to Hegel to Bergson and Heidegger, the argument that time is not the record of unfolding truth but the name of thinking. And what is thinking? Here, explanation. Time is, therefore, not the manifestation of reality or truth, but its (a) production, and there is no way of separating it (which is not an it) from the act of the mind or function. Except, as Derrida reads it, to recognize the dependence of the notion of *ousia* on that of *gramme*, and in Stein, of composition on the performance of writing. Can we say that Stein already *perceives* (recognizes and inscribes) the problematics of time Bergson offered to modernism in the guise of a new metaphysics, a "poetics of symbolism," as we have seen, which we now must read in a way different from, say, Eliot or phenomenological criticism? For Stein, composition goes beyond the poetics of the self-reflexive symbol, to a composition of a "continuous present" that is neither a unified work of art nor the representation of either an authorial intention or a character's stream of consciousness.

Her composition is act, is the act of writing; writing as act, and thus a double-writing, a composing of an open field (an oxymoron) of multiplicities or "tender buttons." Composition is writing *avant la lettre*. Thus Stein's composing of a "continuous present" does not produce psychological narratives. Or, to put it otherwise, it does not conceive of literary writing, least of all the new writing she is at the same time projecting and executing, as an expressive or psychological writing. Her essay cannot describe this writing since it is *"going to be."* And what she calls "beginning again and again" makes of repetition not a figure for the narrative circle, but a figure for the uncanny belatedness of this writing act which has always already begun and is not directed by an authorial subject which is realizing its own identity. (Recall the problematics of identity discussed earlier.) Writing produces a subject-identity only in the form of a name to come, to recall Pound's appropriation of Homer's Elpenor, or Stein's rewriting of authorial identities in her various portraits—like those of Henry James as a general or that of Duchamp (as "Rrose Selevy") inscribed in "a rose is a rose" or that of her maid, where the subject's name no longer needs gender identity and the noun becomes verb (rose, arose). The proper name is an exponential figure, of what is to be.

"Beginning again and again" does not describe a style, but as we have seen names rather a performance of writing. It is writing as self-quotation, whether one points to the repetitions of "a rose is a rose" or to the manner in which Stein's so-called critical and theoretical essays quote her own work, not as examples but as performative "movements" (cf. Bergson) of a writing always already on its way. This performative serves to dissolve the categorical distinctions between the creative and the critical or theoretical, and makes Stein's terminology, as previously noted, not a citation but a use. The performative force of self-quotation makes writing the subject of her texts, and makes her texts self-generating. Thus Stein in *Tender Buttons*, where the thematic is apparently the production of objects by a stripping away of their illusory proper names (the nouns by which they are commonly designated), not only mimes the act of description as a laying bare of the thing, but refocuses the convention of description on the act of writing itself—on the wrist that leads the hand and pen. The shadow of writing is cast by the process. Writing time never effaces the shadow of the hand that leads it, just as the word never becomes transparent or never bears within itself the essence, reality, idea it either names or describes. Writing has always already begun and has never arrived. It has no position. That there is no "there there" in the Oakland of her birth or origin should be no surprise, for there is no terminal there of either life or writing in her theory. If her last words, relative to death, were really, "what is the question," then we may assume they are acts of writing.

The act of writing, then, unveils in a scene that is neither determined nor indeterminate, but which, perhaps not quite in Bergson's sense, moves. Movement is both change and repetition, not without its laws and conditions (contexts which define it, but are in turn opened by its force), but these laws (grammar) can never be fully systematized or theorized. Writing is not without direction, but it is without *telos*. Stein does not make it new simply by positing indeterminacy or by embracing chance. Such metaphors as montage or improvisation do not apply to the time of her writing. And even our effort to call it performative self-quotation, or a kind of self-critical composition or deconstruction can only serve to name an unnamable act which is not an "act of the mind" at all, not an act of an intentional subject but a revisionary undoing or depositioning of the grammatical subject.

Thus what appears to be self-reflexive (and hence modernist) in Stein's writing, the manner in which her texts do not simply quote other of her texts and use them as examples, but proceed by quoting themselves in the act of quotation, distorts and magnifies the artifices of self-reflexivity. Therefore, critical coinages like "continuous present," set over against "prolonged present" (supposedly the unity of narrative succession) or "beginning again and again" as opposed to teleological and genealogical unfolding, do not simply name new formulas for a new narrativity. The in-mixing and dissolving of the notions of space-time in a term like "continuous present" brings into question the apparently natural or real time of traditional narrative, but it does not give us in its stead a new kind of human time. The I of writing is a we, and, to repeat the quotation, "composition is not there, it is *going to be* there and we are here." This is the time of writing.

Writing, then, involves reading, and reinscription. It is both elliptical and irreversible, which means that Stein's repetitions do not simply replicate style nor develop from early to late, but move by a kind of self-insemination and supplementation. There is not progress, clarification, or refinement (*telos*), nor regress as such, in her writing, which is as likely to be narrative in its critical phase as it is alogical and discontinuous in its narrative unfolding (for example, the novel called *The Making of Americans*). Her *Lectures in America* as a case in point stages a critical discourse as a history of the making of American literature, a history of the differentiation of a sui generis force into a national composition that virtually repeats the model of the family history or romance she had earlier recounted in *The Making of Americans*. One may read *Lectures in America* as a literary genealogy which exposes the fictional nature of all nationalistic discourses—that is, of how a nation invents its own language (the fabled "American idiom" sought by Emerson, Whitman, Williams, say) and itself by a kind of creative quotation. Just as *The Geographical History of America* indicated how much of the originality of America depended on the "purloined letter," *Lectures* indicates how the act of quotation neither appropriates nor overthrows the grammar of tradition, but directs itself toward a futural and deferred identity ("*going to be*"). The new idiom to be will not be a cohesive national consciousness so much as the signifier of difference, of "America" as the heterogenous other and American literature as both post- and pre-literary.

In *Lectures*, from its first chapter, "What Is English Literature," to the last, "Poetry and Grammar," Stein enacts a deconstructive intervention upon America's linguistic and literary heritage, the monumental tradition of western narrative which she finds concluded (like the end of history and metaphysics) in the great English literary canon. English literature, she argues, defines itself and the literature of the West in the figure of its geography. This literature, she argues, is a model of clarity

and coherence, which confines itself to representing a "daily island life" (LA, 15). It is a literature saturated by the empirical
tradition, a representational literature of "description simple
concentrated description" that is "shut in with that complete
daily life" (LA, 15,18). Its capacity to totalize and universalize
depends, ironically, on its self-limitation and its appeal to common sense. Its tradition is cognitive, hence its capacity to reconcile "god and mammon," ideality and materiality, in a
moralistic, dogmatic, and formal discourse of ordinary things
and civil manners. English literature, she claims, uses "words to
say something" and is therefore an "indirect" (empirically referential) literature (LA, 23, 24). "American" literature, on the
other hand, is direct and performative: "the thing done and the
doer must be direct" (LA, 24). But a direct literature is not representational, since what is presented is the writing itself, the
doer not as subject but as act. This writing may appear as "confusion," Stein's term for all composition that presents itself
rather than what it refers to, describes, or affirms. And, according to her uncanny history, this confusion of experiment, which
is the characteristic of all originary writing, is modern in the
broadest sense. It began to creep into writing with Shakespeare
and is subsequently complicated in the Enlightenment and Romantic periods only to reach its apocalyptic moment with the
advent of the new century.

Now, one must read Stein's history with a certain eye, recalling the history of language she elsewhere concocts for it: her
notion, to repeat, that the eighteenth century is a time of the
sentence, the nineteenth the period of the phrase (and fragment), and the twentieth the era of the paragraph. It is a literature situated in a culture at war and marked by a style of
"catastrophe." American literature, then, has always been of
this last period, which is not a period. It is different from English literature not simply in the oppositions of order and confusion, but in its separation from the father language, its different
way of choosing and relating words. It is a composing of confusion, made up of old words but in a new grammar. Her America
is not a totalized or composed place, for like her description of
Oakland, there is "no there there." It is only "*going to be*," to recall the phrase in *Geographical History*. One thinks of Williams's

related observation on Poe, the quintessential American writer, whose thereness does not reside in his sense of place but must be found "inside" himself, in an "interiority" that is something other than subjectivity or individual consciousness.[10] Poe's "local" was not local color but the locus of an isolated yet divided self. Poe's literature is an engagement of this crisis *In The American Grain*, just as American literature, for Stein, is "quite alone," its "inside" a form of "separation":

> Think about all persistent American writing. There is inside it as separation, a separation from what is chosen to what is that from which it has been chosen.
>   Think of them, from Washington Irving, Emerson, Hawthorne, Walt Whitman, Henry James. They knew that there is separation a quite separation between what is chosen and from what there is the choosing. (LA, 51)

In English writing, the legislated relation of words (grammar) maps the relations of things. American writing, on the other hand, must compose irrespective of the outside, and "quite alone." It "chooses" to relate things differently. The essays of *Lectures in America* argue that this separation is the issue of the American writers' need for originality and their lack of history. They cannot be nostalgic. They read otherwise, and the title of *Lectures* hints that Stein views her own writing as a kind of interventionist reading. She heralds the experiments of avant-garde art as a revisionary *praxis*, directed upon old conventions, at once analytic and synthetic like that of the cubists in the visual arts. This writing is not marked by style, but by "play" (her word), and its product is a hybrid, never a complete text whose genealogy can be traced to a tradition, but an anthology of quotations and self-quotations that separates this writing out into the other of writing.

Separation is not simply the difference of a new literature from a traditional English literature, but is manifest in the separation of word and referent. American literature has no memory, no history to remember, and no circumscribed reality ("island life") to represent or, reciprocally, give it form. Yet, it is born out of repetition, and what it remembers is the production of the separation. American literature has made its own kind of time, its strange genealogy. Thus, Stein describes her own experiment in writing her family history, in *The Making of Americans*, as a record of a people composing themselves, their general character and individuality, by a kind of repetition-separation: they "said the same thing over and over again with infinite variations," so that in their repeating and her repeating of their repeating there was produced at once a history of a family and a different model of family romance or genealogy (LA, 138–39). As she says of this novel in the lecture entitled "The Gradual Making of The Making of Americans," it is a "question of grammar" (LA, 146). Both lecture and novel, and American writing in general, are autobiographical, not in the sense of recounting a unified life or history, but as a form of self-generating repetition.

Stein displaces the Biblical narrative of "begetting" (genealogical succession) by repetition of an uncanny kind. This is equivalent, she writes, to overcoming the totality of the sentence with the paragraph. Whereas "science is continuously busy with the complete description of something" (LA, 156), a definition she attributes to William James and his argument for pragmatism as against systematic philosophy, the new writing of paragraphs opens the sentence to a different order and direction. Thus *The Making of Americans* was itself a paragraph which she calls, in "The Making of the Making of Americans," a "question of time," of the "essentially American thing this sense of a space of time" (LA, 159–60). The paragraph is repetition, thus autobiographical. Her *Lectures in America* is similarly autobiographical, a composition of new relations, among which are the "relations of a lecturer to his audience" (LA, 205), a recirculation and reinscription of the audience's own language into a different grammar of relations.

"Poetry and Grammar," the last of the *Lectures*, reenacts her undoing of the inherited language, of referential language and the illusion of the noun, a performance she claims to have begun in *Tender Buttons*. Like Williams after her, and as Pound seems to suggest in his and Fenollosa's essay on "The Chinese Written Character," Stein reinscribes the noun as verb, as trope, and proceeds to dissolve the old grammatical hierarchies and privileges into a new diagrammatology. The essay focuses on the way that this deconstructive composition, which she calls poetry, disrupts narrativity and suspends *telos*, undoing the words' apparent semantic grounding in the referent-thing. But her reconceptualization of meaning as an act of writing that produces a new field of meaning-relations ("confusion") does not follow the structuralist substitution of binarism for the old grammar. Her focus, for example, on the significance of syncategoremes—prepositions, articles, and conjunctions—as words of "force," as words which "live by their work" and not by reference, as she says of conjunctions, or her stress of punctuation, of marks which induce the "time" of "confusion" and "mistake" into the text, while producing new relations, anticipates a great many poststructural questions of grammatology. Composition, then, produces "multiplicities," and unveils the heterogeneity of the American family and idiom, the "time of space" and "movement," as she calls it in her Bergsonian terminology: "An American can fill up a space in having his movement of time by adding unexpectedly anything and yet getting within the included space everything he had intended getting" (LA, 224).

Movement, repetition, is self-supplementing, like the performative force of quoting. Composition proceeds in a time of the "One and one and one and one and one," not incrementally, as one plus one, revising itself repeatedly, rewriting itself. This self-quotation is excessive and disfiguring—as she says of her own "poetry," both citing and commenting on "a rose is a rose," this is a "using and abusing" of language, a "using losing refusing and pleasing and betraying and caressing nouns" (LA, 231), an undoing of cognitive and referential language and thus of prose in general:

> Of course when poetry really began it practically included every-thing it included narrative and feelings and excitements and nouns so many nouns and all emotions. It included narrative but now it does not include narrative. (LA, 232)

"Poetry" here names an original and originary language, much as we have seen in Bergson's claims for the privilege of literary to philosophical discourse. But it also names the return of this language out of its alienation. This is a familiar narrative of language, of its fall and return, which we find at the heart of philology, and thus of metaphysics. And Heidegger's reification of *poeisis* and language as the "house of Being" does not escape it, as recent commentators have observed.

Yet, Stein indicates that this return of poetry, as confusion, is not the recovery of an old language of plenitude. Poetry returns by re-turning, not as a primordial originary language but as uncanny repetition, disrupting the repressive laws and linear-circular order of narrative and undoing the old names. American poetry seems to perform a set of changes upon the old paradigms: this "is what made Walt Whitman naturally that made the change in the form of poetry" (LA, 237). Indeed, "America" is the name of this revisionary force, of writing as self-transformation. To repeat, it is "a question of grammar," or more precisely, of re-grammatization:

> Of course you might say why not invent new names new languages but that cannot be done. It takes a tremendous amount of inner necessity to invent even one word, one can invent imitating movements and emotions in sounds, and in the poetical language of some languages you have that . . . Language as a real thing is not imitation either of sounds or colors or emotions it is an intellectual recreation and there is no possible doubt about it and it is going to go on being that as long as humanity is anything. (LA, 237–38)

Language is not a totality, never complete. The new invention is a turning of an old word. Language does not have a history as such, except its entropic movement.

One must always, then, write in a given language, one's mother tongue ("one must stay with the language their language"—LA, 238), but this is different from being dominated by a father language. Writing displaces and recreates the father-noun and its narrative teleology while still maintaining its traces. Writing uses and abuses the noun. Writing is neither paternal nor maternal, but an undoing of the gender difference upon which the master genealogies are based. If one writes in a received language, one might, by a kind of miming, give it a different direction, a new grammar the laws of which cannot now be calculated or generalized. She calls this freedom produced by writing "gay," and in a remark on her text, "Before the Flowers of Friendship Faded Friendship Faded," she defines "gay" as "going back again to a more or less regular form to see whether inside that regular form I could do what I was sure needed to be done and also to find out if eventually poetry and prose were one or not one" (LA, 243). Her portraits, as in *Four in America*, manifest this mimetic disfiguration, turning representational American men like George Washington and Henry James into their other, leaving the disfigured (cubist) portrait in words to indicate the manner in which Washington and James were themselves actors, doers, metonyms for an America which produced itself by separation from Europe.

VI

As we have seen, Bergson's poetics of time, while conducted in a vocabulary overly metaphysical and thus organicist ("creative evolution," "mind and memory," "Creative mind," not to repeat the series of concepts developed around *durée*), also served to question the ground of organicist thinking. Perhaps Heidegger recognized this in his identification of Bergson with a metaphysics the German sought to go beyond, by questioning the intentionality of individual consciousness. Thus, the problem of reading Bergson, as Stein unquestionably did, had also to involve a double reading, an examination of the organicist genealogy and a suspending of the narrative of the father. *Lectures in America*, as we have seen, might be read as such a questioning of literary history, as a narrative of developments within the grammar of western cultural history, in the name of an American writing ("confusion") that is heterogeneous and performative. As I have noted, the novel entitled *The Making of Americans* had earlier retold this story as a different kind of "family romance."

Stein called *The Making of Americans* a "paragraph," stressing the multiple implication of that word, describing it as an allegorization of a nation's genealogical unfolding, as represented in her own family history. I have called this autobiography, but not in the sense of a personal history. Like *The Autobiography of Alice B. Toklas*, it is an autobiography of writing-reading, a story of re-

lated but individually developing destinies that originate out of
the break or separation presented in the novel's very first paragraph: a son dragging his resisting father (and thus the authoritative past) up to and beyond the point of the father's
understanding. The resisting father protests that each genera-
tion should repeat the past routinely. The thrust of the narrative that follows turns this resistance into an uncanny repetition
which reveals, both in theme and style, how each repetition
produces a difference despite the will of the father. A certain
wandering, like that of Melanctha and Jeff Campbell in *Three
Lives*, ensues, as the characters individually and collectively live
and love, repeat the past yet move in different directions, and
toward different destinations. This "loving repeating" (MA,
271) fragments and multiplies the family line, the narrative
line, composing a different kind of genealogical history, exposing the old, self-reflexive conventions of story to an inventive
confusion as the family produces its history in a modern world
to be.

Thus *The Making of Americans* proceeds as an allegory of writ-
ing-resistance, of life as a resistance to and overturning of narrative theory:

> This one that I am now beginning a little to tell about to make the
> fifth one of the six that I am now describing in this explaining of the
> way natures are and are mixed up in men and women, this one had in
> him resisting being and one kind of resisting being only in him and
> not any other kind of nature in him. . . .
> This one was then of the resisting kind in men and women but as I
> was saying, sometimes it is not easy to know it in one whether the being
> of that one is of the resisting kind in them or of the attacking kind in
> them.
> It is not then always easy even after much knowing of some one to
> know whether the being in that one is attacking or resisting, in them.
> (MA, 372–73)

Resistance, here, names a structural and not a psychological
quality of a character's nature. It is, therefore, not repression or
a quality of consciousness, for it describes the relations of individuals to each other, and to the other, rather than the conflicts
of an isolated self or consciousness. The self in its relations, to
others and to the other, is composed like a language, but not in

the Lacanian or structural sense of the resistant signifier. For Stein, human nature and life are composition, like a paragraph. Natures are produced; they are cultivated, hybridized, repetitions with a difference. Americans are made and self-making, in the repetition-compulsion of writing. We write ourselves, one might say, autobiographically.

The making of the American mind, Stein indicates, was not a "slow steadily developing thing" (MA, 372), but an interplay of equivocations, "attacking" and "resisting" which results, as she says of American literature in *Lectures*, in "separation." A family does not unfold in a line or have a completed history, but in its repetitions becomes at once the same and different. Its economy is the economy of writing, an undoing, as Stein says, of the noun and thus of the proper. The displacement of the father-subject neither vanquishes him-it, nor sublates him-it. For this written-writing subject is not self-reflexive. It is not a "substance" but "completely fluid," perhaps in the sense of Bergson's *durée*, except that it is materialized as graphic—thus the paragraph structure, the language of para-graphics. Writing mimes the "substance that is independent dependent beings in so many ways in so many kinds of men and women" (MA, 384). Self and family are both "independent dependent," neither individuals with separate identities nor a collective unity unfolding in a narrative lineage. We Americans are made in paragraphs, not sentences.

The time of the paragraph is not linear or unfolding time, but the time of transition, of translation. Even in a novelistic text like *The Making of Americans*, where a narrative grammar and genealogical order seem to control the story, the effects of repetition, at the level of the sentence, intervene upon the dominant categories, particularly the category of the subject and thus the inside-outside structure of traditional narrative. Stein's novel comments explicitly on this dissolving of categories, the crossing and undoing—and therefore the marginalizing—of the very modes it must employ:

Categories that once to some one had real meaning can later to that same one be all empty. It is queer that words that meant something in our thinking and our feeling can later come to have in them in us not at all any meaning. This is happening always to every one really feeling meaning in words they are saying. This is happening very often to almost every one having any realisation in them in their feeling, in their thinking, in their imagining of the words they are always using. . . . As I was saying categories that once to some one had real meaning come later to that same one not to have any meaning at all then for that one. (MA, 440)

Stein's commentary, here, echoes William James's notion that all science develops by a change of categories and the conceptual vocabulary that designates them. Her notion of revisionary narrative takes a Bergsonian distrust in the old words and categories and turns them into a new genesis or genealogical fable, even though the new categories retain the old names. For Stein does not distrust language, since she gives it no more substance than she gives the "completely fluid" self. Writing works within the old categories of prose, the inside-outside grammar of the determinant word, and the mastery of the subject. But Stein can no longer tell the "tale of the tribe" in the language or categories of the father, of the noun and prose, though she cannot absolutely divest herself of these names and modes. Even in a story like *The Making of Americans*, descriptive narrative seems to be the predominant formal category, even as we watch it being emptied out like the meaning of words Stein's characters feel disappearing or dissolving. What is happening, we might say, is a "question of grammar," an emptying out of the old category of categorical determination. What remains is poetry, to recall a famous line. Thus, such metafictional or self-reflexive commentary as that just quoted works within the novel to reveal the fictions of making, of self making.

Despite the apparent forestructuring of narrative convention, what the reader of *The Making of Americans* reads in/of the novel is the deflection of narrativity, exposing the irreversibility rather than confirming the circularity of such family histories. Just as the Hersland family differentiates itself in multiple lines, no longer controlled by the father (see again the opening paragraph of the unfolding "Paragraph"), the novel itself fragments or multiplies the subject. This is something other than annihilating the subject, or reversing its gender from masculine to feminine, though this also might appear to take place. The emptying out of the old categories, therefore, retains the simulacrum of the narrative-subject or father, but complicates and pluralizes it, not in the name of woman but in the name of writing, as "family living" which is also an existing toward death for "each one." The narrative line is multiple, unilinear and entropic, a doing rather than being—a doing unto death, a resisting of death. Thus the novel's conclusion, which suggests that this resistance of the one who does or acts, though not an overcoming of death and closing of the circle, is the only engendering thinkable:

Family living can be existing and some can come to be old ones and then dead ones and some can have been then quite expecting some such thing. Family living can be existing and some can come to be old ones and not yet dead ones and some can be remembering something of some such thing. . . . Any family living can be one being existing and some can remember something of some such. (MA, 925)

The past as a unity, the father as a substance, does not order the present. Moreover, the individual, the one, is neither individual nor one, as such, for a family is a multiple and not an accumulation of ones. So is a family romance—one + one + one +, on and on.

Categories like story, narrative, novel, and so on, no longer define this writing, this American or modernist writing. Neither do the names "American" or "modernist," nor even the category "poetry." But this emptying out of categories is not nihilism. On the contrary, we are witness to a multiplication of possibilities and thus to a *production of senses*, of different meanings and various narrative lines. I am tempted to call it clitoral writing, even when I know this will be misread as a category of castration in opposition to phallogocentric writing. Yet, for Stein this attack upon the noun, as she describes her effort in *Tender Buttons*, is an extraordinary genealogical intervention, and that text, which she offers as poetry in opposition to the tradition of prose or narrative, may allow us to see that modernism had already passed into postmodernism before it had established itself as the end or closure of tradition. For the terms modernism/postmodernism are only vestigial concepts of an old, philological tradition, that is, of tradition itself as monumental history, the history of the noun.

This "using and abusing," this "caressing and addressing," of the noun in *Tender Buttons*, as she cryptically describes this text in different places, can only be understood as a kind of disseminative or what I am calling clitoral writing. Like much of her work, *Tender Buttons* defies generic categorization, even the name literature itself, appearing as kind of generic distortion and hybrid. It resists formal description, even if one is tempted to employ its three parts as a dialectical triad, or, in a way I find usefully allegorical if logically unconvincing, as a parody of Kantian critique—"Objects" naming the practical or empirical; "Food" the realm of taste or judgment; and "Rooms" the ideality of the pure or categorical. But, then, what we have is almost literally a domestication of the philosophical triad, and a decategorization of the degrammatization of language itself. In *Tender Buttons* Stein first makes the familiar (*heimlich*) unfamiliar (*unheimlich*) and then translates the old names, re-marking things not by the old designations (nouns or signifiers conventionally accepted as proper names) or familiar descriptions but by their strange, incongruous relations. We know objects as congeries of facets, and we know them only in relation to their other. This implies a different grammar and a different sense of categories (rooms), and as such, a strange arrangement of words. *Tender Buttons* situates this play of writing not in the old categories but in the margin, in the transferential zone, without distinct boundaries, of the margin. The section or topic entitled "A Leave," in the section "Objects," marks this disruptive turning of the noun as writing (is "A Leave" one leaf? a leaf of grass? a table leaf? or something left behind, a trait? and so on?): "In the middle of a tiny spot and nearly bare there is a nice thing to say that wrist is leading. Wrist is leading" (SW, 474). There is no naming this thing left behind, this newly revealed leaving, this "tiny spot" or sensitive blank, except in terms of that which opens it to recognition, to its place in the "middle." Is it a remainder, a leaving, or a trait, and what is a leading "wrist"? What is its shadow, especially one that leaves behind a mark or "spot"?

Tender Buttons is centered on this moment of the spot and the middle, and its main thematic concern is that of the "center." Does this center control and organize, or is it always already a signifier from which "The difference is spreading," as the first paragraph of "Objects" says of the "spectacle," the "blind glass" or "carafe" which is a container that does not contain and does not reflect or produce resemblances, but deflects. The objects of *Tender Buttons* are nouns become "tiny spots" or buttons, neither phallic centers nor their castrated absences. They are other than signifiers, but they are sensitive and produce multiple senses. The text opens from these object-spots, these buttons that are not centers, and it proceeds, led by the wrist, or writing, to an increasingly vertiginous "spreading," a dispersion of the center. Indeed, if there is a thematic center to the text, it is the theme of de-centering, "More of double" (SW, 463). The noun is displaced by the "tiny spot," the dividing and divided signifier. From this non-center, as we will see, there spreads, wrist leading, the multiplicities of the letter. This clitoral spot disseminates not semen or semantic authority but a kind of pleasure of the text. In opposition to Rousseau, who found the repetition of writing grounded in empty, unproductive imitation and thus masturbatory guilt, Stein finds in the repetition of writing ("rubbings") a distribution of pleasures ("spreading").

All this is focused on the putative center, and the undoing of the name of the center. If *Tender Buttons* can be read thematically, which is always questionable when Stein's writing is the text, then the themes of center and flower (or centering and flowering, decentering and deflowering) predominate. They belong to a metaphorics of exchange, of translation, or a new economics (grammar) that the text is pressed to articulate. Writing becomes the aesthetics, taste, and judgment of the section called "Food," and begins like breakfast by disrupting the custom of the day's time rather than ordering it. For Stein, "Breakfast" is a strategic break, a custom that interrupts "custom," for "custom is in the center" (SW, 483–84). These buttons or tiny spots, these clitoral points or "dots," newly denominated in "Objects" as the variety of an ordinary, household scene (cups and saucers, tables, carafes, umbrellas, and a hundred other heterogeneous but ordinary things, including containers containing other things), are detached from an order that organizes them and are in turn offered as multiple centers. They are centers that center nothing, nor are they any longer named by their customary proper names.

Thus the concluding section, entitled "Rooms" (and we might observe the domestic category of the room) opens by proposing a reassembling of this multiplicity by a different grammar, one that will contain the spreading without organizing it around a mastering center: "Act so that there is no use in a centre"; "If the centre has the place then there is distribution. That is natural. There is a contradiction and naturally returning there comes to be both sides and the centre" (SW, 498, 499). The act (of writing) *Tender Buttons* is an act of displacement, rather than positioning, but not an act of substitution of one center for another. Nor is it an annihilation of the center. On the contrary, the text produces and proliferates simulacra of the center. It tenders buttons, tiny dots, marks, an heterogeneity of buttons which do not organize a space but transform it: "A centre can place and four are no more and two and two are not middle" (SW, 482). Buttons are tender, but not legal or legislating tender. They do not compose as the middle term, nor can they be sublated. Though Freud called the clitoral button a little phallus, he consigned it, a simulacrum of a simulacrum, to a position outside his economy, as something other than the signifier. The button no longer organizes an economy between the phallus-signifier (for Stein, the noun) and its inverse, the vagina (also nouns, all those receptacles like carafes and boxes which she empties out into unreflective things, the "blind glass" of the first paragraph). Yet the buttons proliferate, multiply senses, or in a contemporary phrase, disseminate an excess of sensation.

One might think of *Tender Buttons* as itself a reading, the reading of, say, a cubist painting, and thus a reading of a reading that disturbs the perspectival grammar of space: "why is there a question and the singularity why is the surface outrageous, why is it beautiful why is it not when there is no doubt, why is anything vacant, why is not disturbing a centre no virtue" (SW, 505–6). Buttons may appear like old names and things, as singularities, but not only do they not center, they call in question the very concept of centering. They no longer have place, or rule over a place. For example, they no longer regulate the phallogocentric economy. They disrupt, proliferate; or like flowers they bloom, but not with organic efficiency or *telos*: "Nothing aiming is a flower, if flowers are abundant then they are lilac, if they are not they are white in the centre" (SW, 508).

Tender Buttons composes rooms full of flowers, without aim. It is a linguistic house of things and words rather than a house of Being, without a central room, a domestic yet *unheimlich* economy that feeds on itself—an American house. In this context, it is ruled, if at all, by the kitchen and the feminine. But one would be mistaken to read this too quickly as an inversion of the masculine. Though the text points out that the "sister was not a mister" (SW, 499), what is at stake in Stein's house of writing is the entire structure of gender difference and thus the metaphysical edifice of the family. The apparently central room is a place of "transfer" and the "tender turn" (SW, 481, 479), a place where "All the stain is tender and lilacs really lilacs are disturbed" (SW, 481), which supplies the house with a fabulous, excessive menu. No longer those emblems of mourning for the lost master, blooming in the dooryard of America's nationalistic crisis, its crisis of identity, these blooms agitate space, open it to a series of unpredictable possibilities, a "choice in gamboling" (SW, 503): "in every space there is a hint of more" (SW, 505).

This disruptive, disseminative force of writing also disturbs and undoes the formal mastery of literature. For Stein, this is what poetry does to masterpieces. But the re-turn of poetry which Stein celebrates in *Lectures in America* is not, as we have seen, the return of a primordial, creative utterance. Rather, as in *Tender Buttons*, it is the return of writing, or more precisely, of the signature. For the button(s) is/are the mark of a disseminating force deregulating the law of narrative. The confusion of this poetry, this writing, disrupts the inside/outside opposition of the book. The button(s) is/are the signature of an "active centre" that is no longer the old phallogocentric signifier, and thus a center in name only: "A whole is inside a part, a part does go away, a hole is red leaf" (SW, 496). This is the penultimate paragraph of "Food," which concludes with a section titled "A Centre in a Table," as follows:

It was a way a day, this made some sum. Suppose a cod liver a cod liver is an oil, suppose a cod liver is tunny, suppose a cod liver oil tunny is pressed suppose a cod liver oil tunny pressed is china and secret with a bestow a bestow reed, a reed to be a reed to be, in a reed to be.

Next to me next to a folder, next to a folder some waiter, next to a folder some waiter and re letter and read her. Read her with her for less. (SW, 497)

Can this reading be read? In "sum," as a sense? Or does it dispatch the *cogito?* Disperse the *sum?* Stein's button, her "reed" is a pen not in hand. It is the folded letter, the mark that makes writing both more and less. It is her fold, the clitoral signature of an American and modernist writing that always already exceeds the categories or genre that allow us to read it masterfully. As a question of grammar, a questioning of grammar, it works within the empty categories of time-space, and thus of Bergson's instrumental language, as a "circular diminisher" (SW, 503), like a writing coming from the future, from the "wrist leading." Both "less" and more, this writing to be is the American identity—a "cod liver," like some c.o.d. that will demand a future payment, more or less. For as Stein repeatedly said of America, how many "acts" make a "play"—"three" at least, or more, to contain "four" saints at least, that excess of "time" which is a dimension not yet calculable.

Chapter Five
The Anomalies of
Literary (Post) Modernism

I

"Modernism" is a word of great currency, almost literally a figure of exchange. But the word itself is hardly definite for being so in vogue, so significant, so obviously figural and in circulation. It is not quite clear or transparent. Nor is it a proper name for either some historical period or some identifiable or unique style. At the same time an historical and an ahistorical category, it *refers* (a term of equal indeterminacy) to the equivocal and irreducible relation between the two. That is, it refers to what is often today called "desire" or the lack that ties any mediation to a dreamed-of immediacy: that which ties the temporal or sensuous to the transcendental or supersensuous, act to idea, and perhaps even literature to philosophy. Modernism is another name for some moment of transition, or for the unnameable and uncanny, an apparently stable term for an instability, which is the reason we are always affixing premonitory signs to it, posting it, as it were, or bracketing it as an historical deviation, at once discontinuous with and supplementary to the tradition, in a way that makes the exception prove the rule. It is not a word, category, or designation which stands alone, nor outside of some historical moment, but it does designate a practice rather than a lapidary or complete form or style. Whatever the modern encompasses, it is an inscription which erases itself, or signifies its own undoing or overcoming. It must, therefore, inscribe the postmodern as surely as it displaces the tradition, by reinscription. Modernism, in brief, and this includes any excess named postmodern which necessarily inhabits it, belongs to criticism, even when it is the name of art or literature. It has become a kind of basic word or concept, in Heidegger's sense of a name that repeatedly undergoes changes of meaning.[1] Strangely, one of its functions is to name that which produces such changes, hence undoes old categories. Modernism names its own anomaly.[2]

Modernism thus understood, as a critical term for criticism, therefore harbors, to repeat, the very crisis it is presumed to reflect and represent, yet repress or overcome. I need not rehearse at this point the familiar debates about it which center upon Mallarmé's essay, "Crisis in Poetry," or the attempts to rewrite this as our "Crisis in Criticism." I will, however, note provisionally Julia Kristeva's observation that a modern scholar of language once claimed that the two most eminent linguists in France were Mallarmé and Artaud, modern poets whose practice detached and highlighted the problematics of the very language they employed self-critically. The implication, that the poets were there before us, before scholarship and criticism, also suggests that the poetic is originally critical, and that it addresses primarily itself. But never directly. And that is the problem, or problematic: for in this address of itself, the language of modernism does not so much achieve self-reflexivity as expose the idealization of self-reflexivity. It submits itself to critical practice. We hear, today, the inflated and hyperbolic claims that the critical is creative or that criticism is poetic, and the equally self-righteous counterclaims of an academic establishment which regales against theoretical critics for writing badly while claiming that criticism is poetic. The debate, however, turns on the acceptance of a division and hierarchy of categories, the privileging of the poetic over the critical, creative immediacy over reflective circumspection, even the imaginative over the discursive: in short, the production and maintenance of an old binarism that modernism, in whatever form it takes, has tended at the same time to perpetuate and undermine. Modernism has never ceased questioning its own privilege, perhaps by way of validating its antithetical practice. Modernism is at best a double-writing: "Literature is now critical," Emerson wrote: "Well, analysis may be poetic."[3] Whether Emerson, Nietzsche, or Valéry, Stevens or Derrida, poetry or philosophy—we have aphorism and anecdote, a double writing, or theory inscribed in practice, wherever modernism appears. We have, that is, apocalypse in the form of catechresis.

Is it possible, then, to define modernism without submitting to its own revisionary force, a force that is just as often conservative as it is radical, but nonetheless irreducible to a monological or ideological discourse? Modernism inscribes its own problematics, but it cannot describe itself. How ironic, then, that modernism as we have come to understand it has always been defined on the model of self-reflexivity when it can be nothing more than a criticism of its modality? In literary history, for example, it has always been the name for some break with or periodic culmination of tradition, and thus some horizon which can be read, but only in two incompatible senses: as end and new beginning. As the latter, it would be at once a return to origins and originary. That paradox marks a good deal of what we recognize as the primitivism or neo-primitivism of modernism, the ahistoricity and immediacy it claims, just as it supports the sense of a continuum or historical totality. Modernism thus belongs, and does not belong, to the eternal return and the hermeneutical circle. That is, it gestures some exception to and of the rule, a certain unruliness; yet it cannot be said to be outside the law. That is why it can only be defined by some other character—by its excess, by the postmodern, or as we will see, by the *figural*, by style, but style now thought of as that which presents itself to the eye and at the same time resists perception or reading. Not style in the singular, then, but styles, irreducible heterogeneity.

Critics such as de Man and Lyotard, although not easily reconciled to one another, seem to agree that the problematic of the modern is located in figurality. Each rejects the term "modern" as a designation of a period, such as its use by historians to set the modern Renaissance against antiquity, though even here the notion of Enlightenment implies a certain priority of self-reflection and thus humanist privilege. As a comprehensive term, however, modernism signifies not only something close to us in time, the *now* and the *new*, but something that re-marks itself in two senses: that comments on itself, and that under-scores its technical and abstract properties or those devices that it uses to produce meaning and structure. Simply, modernism seems to be inseparable from self-reflection and self-reflexivity. Even when it is employed in a neo-Marxist fashion by critics like Fredric Jameson to suggest both an historical and structural map of recent history—as a dialectic of tradition/highmod-ernism/postmodernism superimposed upon the economic his-tory it represents, as commodity—the word-concept is troubled by its appeal to the question of style(s) and hence by a double-ness. For style indicates not only a formal, abstract, and visible mark but also that which conceals the very thing that produces it. Style(s) presents itself to perception and interferes with per-ception. Its figurality is visible and corporeal, and irreducible to a narrative account of things. The modern at once shows itself, and withholds itself from (re)presentation. It is commodified and employed speculatively, as a capitalized value, but it also tends to escape its appropiation and to skew those same values for which it apparently stands.

This is why it is difficult to discuss the modern and the post-modern without reference to the visual arts, or even architec-ture, as organizations or constructions of space. Yet this construction is no less a critique or deconstruction of spatiality. It inevitably disrupts representation or perspectivism (hence il-lusion) and offers up an irreducible image or figure that paro-dies its own status. It tends to open the space or mark the artifice of its closure. If one wishes to maintain the question within the field of verbal arts, then figure, as in Mallarmé, in-volves that organization of marks on the page which are not in-dicators of meaning, not even signs, yet call attention to themselves as the *abgrund* of any possible meaning. The mod-ern demands to be read in some literal sense, because it in-scribes marks which suggest an organization of signs that can be decoded. What if the signs it organizes are themselves signs re-ferring to a twofold nature of signs? That is, signs occupy and organize space yet prevent our reading that space (conceptual-izing or narrating it). In one important sense, as deconstructive (postmodern) critics have argued, the organizational or cre-ative force would be located in the equivocal relation of marks that bear no semantic load, but appear to the eye as figures that unfocus and fracture the scene, provoking interpretation or reading by resisting meaning. They indicate, these indicators, that something cannot be repesented. They present the unpresentable or indicate an inexpressible meaning. Thus, they undermine their own role as fetish by highlighting the relation between form and fetishism.

Certainly, since French symbolism we have had to consider modernism in terms of heterogeneity that at once summons us to understanding, luring us to read things in terms of what the old words meant while reminding us that some aberration appears there, that something is not reducible to conceptualization. De Man formulates this as the rhetoricity of literary language, the *aporia* that joins the cognitive or meaningful stance of figure (trope) to a performative or persuasive function that subverts meaning. Generalizing this beyond literary figuration, Lyotard employs the equivocal opposition of *discourse* (narrative or story, *récit*) and *figure* (or that which resists induction into the flow of discursive meanings). Figurality appears and marks itself not as the appearance of a withheld meaning, but as a phantasm or unaccountable image.

By way of talking about criticism or a certain *praxis*, we have drifted from reflection on the idea of the modern to some postmodernist or deconstructive inflections of it. In other words, according to Lyotard, this literature-art, as well as being self-critical, itself performs a critical or disruptive function. It is the artists themselves who insist that their art is critical, even apocalyptic, in that its performance affects itself at the most basic levels of form or medium. What does it mean, then, to say that literature is critical, or modern literature self-critical, and yet to assert that modernism (and postmodernism) are not and cannot be purely self-reflexive, as they have traditionally been defined: that, to the contrary, they are disturbances of speculation and thus of the illusion of presence, of representation? Modernism tends to offer itself as illustration, but only to illustrate its own mechanics, thus presenting or exposing the *technē* of representation.

Modernism, I will argue, and with it anything we can designate as postmodern, is complicated and problematized by this question of illustrative figurality. If a modern work of literature is that which reflects or comments on itself, this meta-poem can only be understood in a critical way, as a cata-critical act. But in what sense can poems, or literary works in general, be said to act or perform? In what sense does the term "speech acts" depend on an idea of metaphoricity, and thus mark itself as a trope of trope? What is involved when we begin to tell a story of literary history as the influence of an earlier work on a later, or as the anxiety of influence which produces a later work's revision of the first, producing a catachresis that seems without end or beginning? I am echoing Bloom here, because he is rightly celebrated for developing a new and certainly extravagant sense of literary history as an open and endless criticism, a criticism of criticism by literature. But Bloom tells his story in terms of romanticism, to which the modern is no more than an "ephebe's" twist. Yet, Bloom has to have recourse to a new model of language, of rhetoricity and tropology, the inescapable model for any modernism. It is just this inescapable model, I will suggest, that puts in question the dream of modality and method, that disrupts the model of self-reflection, that we have to consider in reflecting on the "critical function of the modern." In Bloom's view, modernism is just another name—and an historically deviant one—for this tropological economy of Romanticism, while "romantic" is a generic name for poetry itself, for its Nietzschean capacities of self-overcoming, of displacing the truth with "lie."[4]

II

Any definition of the modern—self-consciousness, self-reflexivity, experimentation—must acknowledge its claims of difference, its posture of uniqueness, of the new which nevertheless can only be defined against convention and received styles. In Eliot's terms, tradition seems always to regulate "individual talent." Formalism, but a new form; spatiality, but a new organization of space—these signs of a material or sensuous construction accentuate the modern as the ultimate technical refinement, as *technē*, as work and object rather than living organism.

Thus the modern is always less and more than what it putatively completes. One is reminded of the American New Critics' efforts to reconcile the ideal of organic form, derived from Kant through Coleridge, with the technical abstractions of an industrial and even post-industrial age; to preserve, let us say, in the pure crystal of aesthetic and verbal space a self-reflexive operation that mirrored the purity of a transcendental consciousness or divine imagination. This contradiction of sensuous and supersensuous which haunts aesthetics from Plato or Platonism to Kant and Coleridge, and even Hegel, and is reversed but not overcome by Nietzsche (nor for that matter, finally, by Heidegger), is the reigning problematic of the modern. It is everywhere reflected in the ethic of nostalgia that haunts modern criticism, the simultaneous protest against the dehumanization of art and praise for its technical expertise, its crystalline abstraction. Modernism's preoccupation with space or the potentiality of closed space—whether in the self-reflexive poem or functional architecture or non-representational painting or non-serial music—inevitably mixes the metaphors of the organic and the technical, life and death.

In the effort to resolve the form-content and space-time dichotomies that perplex western aesthetics, modernism can only overcome the crisis by exacerbating it. One could demonstrate this thematically in poems as conventionally modern as Hart Crane's *The Bridge* or Ezra Pound's *Cantos* as well as in the self-conscious nativism of Wright's architecture: works which incorporate what Heidegger calls the "discordance" or contradiction of western aesthetics as surely as does any so-called dehumanized art, for example, analytic cubism, surrealism, or any of the arts now grouped under the generic term "postmodern." This is what allows a postmodern criticism in general, particularly a critic like Lyotard, to argue that every modernism is already inhabited by a postmodern discordance, or by certain configurations or marks which signify at the same time the work's double claims, to closure and development, thus to a unity that is not at the same time abstract and dead. Strangely enough, it is this apparently non-living technical force, signified by functions within the work which accentuate their artifice, that marks the productive potential of the modern: that is, it breaks up or opens the modern, or signifies the modern's will to power or will toward closure. In Nietzsche's terms, art "lies," but in accentuating its illusion, it displaces "truth." In remarking its lie, it is more truth than that which perpetuates illusion. Lyotard thus employs the periodic term "postmodern" to name this function of differential production, this disrupting intervention of a figure that cannot be reduced to the conceptual understanding of discourse or narrative representation. This *différend*, as he names it, signifies the play of the postmodern within the modern, and allows him to claim, as we will see, that the postmodern is necessary for the modern to come into its own, or for it to appear. This is the critical function or force that the work bears within itself, a sign of its double-ness or heterogeneity, the "double writing" that pervades all discourse and disallows our generic distinctions between the creative and the critical.

Gilles Deleuze denominates modernism in literature, in this case narrative literature, as the working of a "divergent series" against the rule of narrative, which he calls the "rule of convergence." Whereas narrative pushes themes toward resolution, the modern mode disperses and reweaves or imbricates irreconcilables. Montage is not quite the name for this *imbricolage*. Thus Joyce's "continually decentered chaos" in *Finnegans Wake* becomes a "power of affirmation" in keeping a series open, and like a "literary machine" produces an "internal reverberation" or resonance of oppositions that resists any closure of the narrative line.[5]

We find in these descriptions of a postmodern activity disturbing the representational or the descriptive, a strange kind of practice that makes the critical discourse in effect repeat, as if by parody, the creative. Criticism can only speak theoretically from the (dis)advantage point of its own practice, since what it must do is produce a new descriptive language for that which resists description. Deleuze calls this the "constitutive inequality" of every work. Equivocality, heterogeneity, heterology, and in the more extreme sense, the non-concepts (not exactly neologisms or solecisms) of Derrida—*différance*, and so on—emerge as an aberrant lexicon from beneath what has seemed a normative if not natural aesthetic language.[6] In one way or another, these effects disturb the eye and ear, and touch the senses, recalling a certain non-sense at the constitutive center, which is no longer a center at all. We have learned to accept this figural irrationality in what we recognize as the work of art, but when it appears in the critical domain to comment on the impossibility of theory, or to disrupt the logic of mastery or totalization, it must be marginalized. When criticism threatens to preempt art's access to the "other," criticism must be exempted. But if criticism as such is already inscribed in the artwork, or is literary, then it can only be exempted by ignoring its function and returning criticism to its ordinary and subordinate role of thematic elaboration. This is the claim made for meta-literature: that it sufficiently accounts for or thematizes itself.

To accentuate the discordant function of criticism in modern (or postmodern) art, on the other hand, calls attention to certain limits within our old sense of reading: reading precedes and suspends interpretation, or the recovery of meaning. It also calls attention to a certain *mise en abyme* structure that inhabits modernism, and suggests that this critical modernism in some way affects all literary discourse and is simultaneously effaced by literary history. This is obviously too broad a generalization: that literature is never original but originary, that it begins in the moment when it is forced to reflect on itself, when it, in effect, signifies its departure from myth (Bakhtin) or from the direct interpretation of truth and signifies its own figurality and modality. In this sense, the appearance of Achilles's shield in the *Iliad* and Penelope's tapestry in the *Odyssey* would be allegories of the advent of literature itself. Penelope's nightly unweaving, like Scheherazade's interrupted narratives, is a story of narrative's delaying mechanism, or productive deferral, a story of story which recent postmodern literature like that of Nabokov, Pynchon, John Barth, and others, repeats in extremis by following out a logic parody. Borges's story of Pierre Menard's rewriting of *Don Quixote* brackets the entire history of the novel within this novelty of repetition, and, like Nabokov's *Pale Fire*, stages the novel as the most critical of genres because it has advanced most effectively and forcefully by putting genre in peril. Criticism and death are the necessary conditions for literature to come into being, or for the idea of being to appear as representation. One finds it difficult to understand a history of .

the novel that does not also subvert itself, though the intertextual relations between narrative forms are not without some rule. But it is the writing of this rule that poses so many questions, a scene Henry James staged in his Prefaces as the problem of rereading, revising, and reseeing. Could one say that James marks and re-marks his own invention of a certain realism as a critical act directed against both the "romance" and the Flaubertian displacement of the old representational illusion? The Prefaces restore to our awareness the technical operations of a figurality we may call critical in that they call attention away from the meaning of the representations to operations themselves, and show us the revisionary mode of the technical operations.

In describing the works of modernism, then, we will have to confront the question Derrida posed in *Post Card*, at a point where he is talking about the discourse of philosophy, or, more specifically, of the post-philosophical claims of a social science like psychoanalysis to overcome the theory-praxis problematics. His example is Freud's use of the example, or the crux introduced into any system when the so-called method of analysis is also part of that which is to be analyzed—where the family romance or Oedipal complex becomes the general pattern for understanding, analyzing, and correcting a condition which it also names:

> What occurs when acts or performances (discourse or writing, analysis or description, etc.) are part of the objects which they designate? When they can be given as examples of precisely that of which they speak or write? Certainly, one does not gain an auto-reflexive transparency, on the contrary. A reckoning is no longer possible, nor is an account, and the borders of the set are then neither closed nor open. (391)

According to Derrida, the ideal of self-reflexive transparency has always been the dream of western metaphysics or the philosophy of (self-) presence, evident in its arguments for systematization and closure, totalization and mastery. But the dream of truth, and desire for theory that at once inaugurates and governs a practice that completes it, have only been sustained by a strategic effacement and seamless reconstruction of the narrative and figural modes this discourse had to employ. To expose this self-referential and self-justifying discourse, then, to deconstruct it or submit it to something like a postmodern analytic, cannot be done from the outside, but only from a certain margin that characterizes the discourse itself. This new critical discourse, however, can no more inhabit, parody, and overcome the old work, by exploiting its own parasite, than it can escape its own limits. That is, the analytic of exposure, of ex-position, is implicated in the game (*jeu*). This limitation affects every inscription, and is indeed the source of the productive power of all discourse.

If there is a post-philosophical discourse or (human-) scientific methodology at all, its authority derives from these limits and not from its capacity for overcoming them. According to Derrida, this applies as well to the pure language of mathematics as well as to the pure word of poetry, a problematics inscribed in Godel's theorem which, ironically, has enhanced as much as it has threatened progress in its quest for a *principia mathematica*. The questioning of a referentiality and self-referentiality, which has seemed to belong to a certain (marginal) philosophy of language, is something inscribed in discourse itself, and not something that has emerged with the nihilism and skepticism of a post-Cartesian modern age or, more recently, with the "revolution of the word" in the nineteenth century. Criticism cannot begin outside of what it criticizes, hence can never account for the present or future condition of that which it is a part. It cannot, therefore, provide the trajectory of a destination—what the thing it studies/analyzes will be—any more than it can account fully for a present condition in which it participates. True enough, the ideal of self-reflexivity achieves its essential expression in the Hegelian formulation, as subsequently underscored in such reversals as Nietzsche, Marx, Freud, and Heidegger. But these reversals could never be simple reversals, but only indelible re-markings of the heterogeneous field of the ensemble. The power of post-Hegelian discursive practices resides in the limits of the very metaphysics they expose, and thus in their own limits. In its self-exposure, its *posture* as pure science.

We have seen, in recent years, the attempt to write a history of literary modernism in terms of a post-Romantic poetics, or as the achievement of a purity (from *Symbolisme* to post-symbolist reversal) of the word, that is, as a turn toward language through which literature realizes self-reflexive transparency, the systematic closure that metaphysics could only dissimulate. Thus we have a history which runs dialectically from Romanticism to Modernism to Postmodernism, through what one current journal (*boundary 2*) celebrates as a negative or open dialectic of overcoming: a progressive history of demystification which recounts literature's withdrawal from history and from the sickness of the romantic self, into itself, into an hermetic purity that orders the play of the sign within the restricted or closed economy of the symbol. The postmodern, then, becomes that moment not only of reversal but re-turn, a venting of this closure, or fracturing of the mirror and its illusion of transparency. Focusing on the impenetrability of its reflecting surface, which is something like the irreducible corporeal figure that resists understanding, the postmodern would in this account open a closed field and return to reality and history, not as representation or mirror but as productive or resistant performance. This particular literary history, of literature's closure of history and its return to history, has been variously applied: to the broad movement beyond romanticism, or to the continental developments from Flaubert and Mallarmé through Lautréamont and surrealism to Borges and the parodic deconstruction of literature. *boundary 2* recounts it in the economy of two modernist moves: boundary 1 referring to either Virginia Woolf's or Ezra Pound's date of 1910 as the beginning of the modern; boundary 2 naming Charles Olson's proclamation of 1950 as the beginning again of the new or postmodern. It is not surprising that this kind of history comports with the economic history described by Fredric Jameson and other neo-Marxist critics, even though Marxism does not confer the same privilege upon postmodernism as does a theory that celebrates literature's self-overcoming, its going beyond aesthetics, as it were.

Strangely enough, postmodern writers tend to discount this privilege, even as they acknowledge that they work self-referentially to parody, disturb, and generally open the hermetic enclosure of literature, without, as Heidegger evidences, indulging in a nostalgia to get back to some pure essence of the poetic being. If, as Charles Olson wrote, the modern/postmodern poet must "go back" behind the self-consciouness of western literature, he or she must go back "to come forward." Or as John Barth has argued, if postmodern literature must "exhaust" literature, or parody it to the point of showing its exhausted resources (its becoming modern, in the sense of becoming at the same time purely formal and thematically nihilistic), the logic of parody, or what I will call genre-cide, is necessary as a surgical maneuver and not an end in itself.[7] But the undoing of the modern cannot be simply another version of nostalgia, the quest for some kind of primitive power, Dionysiac ground of life, or even pre-Socratic wisdom of Being, as in Heidegger, any more than it can, as avant-garde, lead the advance, or in the utopian sense, achieve the advance of a literature that would put literature on some new ground or topos, some position that would include both life and history. In sum, such privileging of the postmodern simply tends to repeat the metaphysics of the humanist literary tradition, whether in the triumphs of rebellion or nihilistic despair.

Rather, what we now call postmodern can no more be decisively separated out from or placed in advance of the modern than can the modern be seen to complete or sublate the tradition. The crisis rests in the history, or in the inescapable need of the modern/postmodern to account for itself: to place itself in and beyond history, to give itself a history, to account for history but also for a literature which is at the same time in/beyond history. This is what is implied by such projects as de Man's effort to rewrite the history of romanticism, and, oppositely, by Bloom's attempt to rewrite all literary history as a version of romanticism or "quest romance." Literary history, then, is inseparable from criticism, but not simply in the sense that criticism is a discursive practice that accounts for the ontological or cognitive status of literature, its representational role in a history of ideas. Deconstruction's undoing of the cognitive and generic borders between literature (poetry) and criticism (thought) can no more escape the problematics of self-reflexive acts or performances in literary criticism than it can escape the double-bind of philosophical discourse in general. In Harold Rosenberg's oxymoronic title, *The Tradition of the New*,[8] we may find inscribed the entire problematics of accounting for the new and original, especially as it highlights the dilemma of belatedness and even entropy (signified in the changing sense of energy and, more recently, communication theory over the last century) that perplexes yet animates the (post)modern revolution and its counter-practices. The new can only proclaim its futur-ology figuratively (prophetically and apocalyptically) from the position of its death.

III

If literary history is in a sense nothing other than a history of criticism, written by and as criticism, and if literature contains an inextricable critical element or an element of self-account-ability, it follows that literary history will be composed of a set of readings (not necessarily interpretations) which resist narrative closure and even full accountability. Such histories tend to resolve into themes or thematic stories, threads whose counterpoint is never fully resolved, despite the efforts to reconcile themes around one or more dominant motifs; that is, to recount the whole in the part. This effort to overcome what we might call the Godelian indeterminant, to make an element in the set account for the entire set, is clearly exemplified in the problematics of writing the history of national literature: say, American literature. Of course, we have risked here the irrational example of the example, of the exemplary case. Nevertheless, one might argue that American literature, as well as the various attempts to write a history of American literature as at once a unique literature yet a part of the history of western literature, is a case in point. An instance of the inherent contradiction from Emerson to the present, the American writer's effort to pronounce the possibility of an American literature, to clear a space for it, has tended not so much to produce that new literature as it has made it possible for criticism to write a history of that desire. Thus Emerson joins with Bloom in that enterprise, while traditional literary history proceeds as if its task of description addressed a unique history and an authentically different literature which, nevertheless, it could recount in terms applicable to any national literature. These terms include a literature at the same time new yet a chapter, perhaps the last and latest chapter, of the West, characterized by its own nativist elements, by a continuity of themes and forms, for example, the need to produce its own epic, an ancient genre, within a modern idiom. In sum, these histories tend to efface the very contradictions, the very "discordance," as Heidegger calls it, which is essential to the new or to art in general—its own critical force or capacity to deconstruct received structures. Ironically, American literary histories tend to tell a normative story about an exceptional case, or at least about a literature that repeatedly insists on its need to be exceptional. American literature, that is, problematizes any history that might be written about it, but it continues to provoke efforts to write that history. The provocation, interestingly enough, seems often enough to reside not in the work's account of its failure and frustration, but in its ironic inability to account for its failure to account for itself. Sometimes it seems to write a history of its own future: visionary, prophetic, exceptional, and different, therefore instigating its own interpretation by a clearing of the ground of past references. In this regard, one might argue that American literature in general seems to conform only to Bakhtin's broad definition of the novel, which differs from the epic in the sense that it is a strictly historical and ceaselessly self-revising or open genre, in contrast to the epic's preoccupation with a completed, unchanging, and even mythic past. Whatever the genre, American literature—and by this I now designate that literature which in effect reflects upon itself, and on its own limits or failure to realize itself, rather than a literature written in America or that literature which seems to represent, or even invent, "American" themes like Adamism—is like Bakhtin's novel, self-revisionary, rather than visionary, and prophetic only in the sense that it is "prospective" rather than "retrospective," as writers from Emerson to Olson have proposed.

The familiar attempts to write in American literary history according to its distinct themes—Adamism, Paleface and Redskin, the frontier—have never failed, even in the arguments for a fundamental nativism or primitivism, to suggest that this return to origins had to be made through the self-conscious methods characteristic of modernism. There is no more classic example of this than Charles Feidelson's groundbreaking *Symbolism and American Literature* which concludes with a postscript announcing: "[T]he affinity between large areas of American literature and of modern literature brings to light unsuspected aspects of both," that affinity being particularly evident in what they share with a broadly defined symbolist movement in modern thought.[9] Feidelson's is a stiking piece of critical reading, but a curious history, which argues that symbolism has supplanted "romanticism and realism" or "idealism and materialism" in the sense that it is a humanism, but a "critical humanism." Thus, he begins one step beyond Matthiessen whose own canonical text had placed the American tradition at the end of or in the aftermath of the Renaissance, itself a repetition and fulfillment of that theory of language Emerson found in Coleridge as filtered through Kant. Both Feidelson and Matthiessen locate this humanistic rebirth in Eliot's particular notion of the modern as an escape from the abysses of romantic dualism (though Eliot had found humanism only another version of the romantic).

No matter the question of precursors and influence, it is the role given to individual talent, and to the problems visited upon the American writer, both by his lack of a past and isolation, that Feidelson, like de Tocqueville, discovers to be at the heart of an American literary tradition that has had to invent itself anew by a kind of auto-reflection. American literature was virtually born in crisis, its legacy the self-consciousness that haunted western thought in its latter-day moments, in romanticism and Hegelianism. Symbolist theory, from that Eliot had found in the French literary scene of the nineteenth century to the philosophical symbolism of Bergson and Cassirer, signified the overcoming of Cartesian dualism. It was not, however, a philosophical resolution so much as a displacement of philosophy by aesthetics and theology. Symbolism, as Feidelson argued, was a "theory of knowledge" reconciling history and ideas, and thus an aesthetic figure which verified the old theology by bringing its form once more before our eyes. The "autotelic" poem of Eliot signified and made manifest the resolution of that "double consciousness" or Cartesian dilemma inherited from the Renaissance and exacerbated by every argument that attempted to master it, the latest being romantic pathos and existentialist despair. Indeed, all of that history of renaissance as self-consciousness could be resolved in a post-Hegelian reification of the symbol over the sign, a belief in the present-ness of the symbol which could harbor two-in-one, a displacement of romantic irony by humanism.

But whereas the New Criticism had followed Eliot in discovering this symbolist resolution in poetry or the lyric form, albeit a lyric like Donne's, structured according to drama or dramatic oppositions extended in time but resolved in form and figure, Feidelson discovers his symbolist model to be a narrative. In this he owes a considerable debt not only to the Warburg philosophers but to Joseph Frank's formulation of the modern novel as "spatial form," modeled upon Worringer's aesthetics. Feidelson's metatext is Gide's *The Counterfeiters* which he reads in the spirit of the *mise en abyme,* only to discover that the artist himself has, following Mallarmé, effected a way of closing the text's self-references upon themselves, thus effacing the question of just where the original and unreflected moment might stand (whether outside or inside, in history or in experience, in action or consciousness). The aesthetic unity of the symbol realized in the metanarrative sufficiently accounts for itself. Self-criticism brings itself to completion, or stops all drifting towards the abyss of non-meaning opened up by narratives about narrative. Melville's *Pierre* is at once an earlier and weaker version of this aesthetic sublation, a much more awkward work of art but nevertheless an exemplary form of modernism in its anguished self-reference and self-questioning. This self-questioning is the sign of critical humanism, or at least the sceptical stage of it, the other position being reflected in the extravagant optimism of Emerson's organic theory of language. Feidelson, in sum, passes through the uncanny moment of any self-reflexive text to accept the triumph of the modern in the aesthetic detachment dramatized at the meta-level. Pierre's inability to reconcile action and reflection calls our attention to the form of the novel itself rather than the pathos of its characters. Thus, the work itself achieves a unity it cannot allot to its individual characters or to the individual of democracy in general, particularly the democratic writer condemned to be a representative man.

Now, recent readings of both Gide and Melville have turned this narrative of self-reflexive closure into another story. This newer criticism goes by the name of postmodernism, and sometimes deconstruction, and in its thrust constitutes a massive attack on nostalgic formalism, theories of closure, and totalized criticism. There is no time or point here to rehearse those readings, nor to defend their strategies, except to claim that what goes under the name of poststructural criticism appears itself in the disturbing forms of that modern literature it would take as model.[10] Or in other words, by taking modern self-reflexive literature as a model, the New Criticism produced an effect similar to that which Derrida examines when he asks what occurs when "acts or performances" become a part of that which they designate. Criticism has only to recite the anomaly of the case as it works within the double language of the self-reflexive discourse, no matter what the form, poetic or narrative. It concludes that self-reflexivity, far from being the figure that might account for the unity of the text, is itself the figurative place where "constitutive inequality" must be located. In brief, it has only to accentuate the critical force of the text, whether one wants to (mis-)name it postmodern or modern. I will therefore turn to some examples, keeping always in mind Derrida's Heisenbergian (or Godelian?) waning of the inseparability of the act of analysis and what is analyzed. Like Wallace Stevens's "Connoisseur of Chaos" (215), which begins with a contradictory formulation and then offers "Pages of Illustrations," illustration does not define but becomes a part of the critical act itself, that "act of the mind" which elsewhere serves for Stevens as the figure of the modern.

IV

Modernism simply cannot conceive of itself, or be defined in opposition to its other, either tradition or the postmodern. It is the very name of an anomaly, and of what links theory and prac-

tice in a double discourse. Charles Olson is by his own proclamation a postmodern, in revolt against the "high modernism"
of Eliot and Pound. In his criticism as in his poetry, he defines
the second "boundary" of a still newer or post-Imagist, post-ob-
jectivist poetry, which he calls "projective" (one might hear, at
this point, in the *pro* a sign of a recurrent American project, as
in the Emersonian "Prospects" that ends *Nature*, and the rejection of "retrospective" thought which opens it). I have elsewhere had occasion to examine the problematics of Olson's
self-defined "field theory" as it amends Pound's and Williams's,
so I will only repeat here Olson's charge, itself repeated in deconstructive criticism, that it is necessary to ventilate a stag-
nated modernist tradition, which is humanist and logocentric,
by exposing its reactionary presuppositions. Thus Olson's inaugural gesture is to reject the immediate past and to repeat, albeit with a difference, the modernist gesture.

Olson calls the western tradition "Mediterranean," and finds
that it oscillates between the values of a mimetic (objective) and
an expressive (subjective) literature without recognizing the
impasse of either. In contrast, what he names "projective" (also
objectivist) poetics defines literature as action, manifest in a de-
liberately non-representational practice that would expose the
powerful dissimulative and repressive techniques of a classical
humanist tradition. Like Heidegger and Derrida, Olson calls
the logocentric tradition totalitarian and ideological, and finds
its representational operations lurking everywhere, even in the
attempts of Pound and Williams to make it new. Like Pound, he
argues that literature must return to history, but this cannot be
a simple turn, since history is not the history of a becoming or a
telos, nor a reflection on and representation of events, but is the
event of a culture organizing itself as space, or organizing
space. He would ultimately define poetry as "document," meaning that poetry is an assimilation and articulation of the fragments or records, the signs, by which any culture realizes its
structural coherence, particularly its systems of communication
and exchange, and thus becomes a culture. In this sense, a culture begins (though it always begins a second time) with its invention of writing, with its marking out of differences and its

production of value through exchange. A poetics of "document" is irreducibly historical, but not metaphysical.

Beginning, as beginning again, always occurs in the space between two cultures, or a place of crossing, the borders between cultures: for example, ports of call or agoras of exchange. The heroes of a culture would be those who effected these transitional exchanges, who in "going back" to "come forward," as Olson puts it, would not simply import old values into a new scene but would enact a transvaluation of values. These are the figures who invent the means of communication and the modalities of distributing knowledge to others. They function as performatives, not bearers of a fixed cognitive value. In a sense, every culture's history is a repetition, not of the substance or even pattern of the past, but of its struggle to define itself. The invention of writing was the first mark of difference, and of disjunction, but also of the possibility of communication and exchange, measurement and transformation. In the repetitions and discontinuities of history, every culture is initiated by marks or signs that, whatever their resemblance to the marks and signs of other previous cultures, have different meanings from what they might in another context. Compare, but also contrast, he would say, Mayan glyphs with Egyptian hieroglyphs, but do not assume they are the return of the same, a kind of arche-writing. Though the religious space of both may be signified by pyramidal structures, their practices are not necessarily identical. What remains in the artifacts, the styles, of a culture is the evidence of a will to order, and this is grounded in communication and exchange of signs. But meaning-value does not reside in the signs (cargo) themselves; on the contrary, value is altered and produced in their use. Similarly, relations between present and past cultures could exist only in this transformational repetition. History does not advance, but one still must think of some point of transition between early and late. What is needed is a new model or language of transformation like that Riemann provided for mathematics in the nineteenth century in order to account for the relations between two otherwise discontinuous planes, what Riemann called "multiplicities." Poetry, for Olson, would enact something like this new mathematic, or even a new geo-metrics, in which old signs are carried over into new uses. The poem must think this point of transformation and exchange in both temporal and spatial terms. One reflects on the past not to appropriate its fixed values, but to understand the laws of its dynamic, its capacity to produce and distribute variety. Decoding and translating a lost language would not so much retrieve the meanings of the culture as reveal the laws of exchange: just as signs carried over from one culture to another change value in the new culture, like or similar signifiers (cognates) transported across space and time produce or instigate meanings not immanent in the sign. Cultures always have some medium of exchange, but neither signified nor signifier is continuous or stable.

If poetry is a kind of linguistic document, a mapping of transactions, its project is revisionary and not representational. Now, I have indulged myself here in a kind of transaction between Olson's terms and those of deconstruction, but have not radically distorted his formulations of a counterpoetics. For Olson, a poem is a transaction between people or, as he says, between two differences separated yet related by that permeable but differentiating surface of the skin. Olson does not think of the self as a subjectivity, an inside, connected to the outside or the other by a network of receptors and transformers (nerve ends) translating sensation into proper concepts. The skin is a dividing yet interrelating surface, a medium where sense in both senses is exchanged, transformed—a point in the communicative transaction that is much like Deleuze's *topos* of "constitutive inequality." The skin is not properly between, a demarcation, yet in a strange way it is the indefinable and equivocal place of all crossing, the place of linguistic interface.

Language is thus the medium of exchange and ground of culture, a ground that is not a ground but an *abgrund*. Like the poststructuralists, Olson finds language inextricable from writing or the graphic, and despite the repeated celebrations of voice in his criticism, voice names the temporality of measure or line, hence spacing and/or a certain figural modality. Voice for Olson is producible like a voice imprint or musical score. Writing, then, is not for Olson phonetic, any more than the glyph is a natural representation. A glyph is a mark or sign of a transaction; it is a heterogeneity of signs. Like Derrida's (non) concepts of the *mark* and *trait*, or Lyotard's and de Man's stress on a figurality that will not be reduced to meaning, Olson's glyph at once signifies and withholds signification. It can be perceived but not fully appropriated as meaning. It provokes one to read, to interpret, to act, but never to complete or close it. A glyph is the spatial inscription of an action, just as an act was necessary for it to be cut literally into stone. As in Stevens's supreme fiction, it is both abstract and changing. Strangely, uncannily, the signifying mark signifies nothing, yet is the *abgrund* of signification. The measure or mediating mark becomes the decentered center of a productive activity:

I figure this swims up, now, this business of noun as graphic Ist, allowing for narration afterwards, the double function, man makes noun then makes verb, because, such activity, such transposition, is, at root, I figure, as process, to what constitutes glyphs.[11]

For Olson, the glyph is a metonym for poem, a means of communication and not a closed work reflecting (upon) itself. And it is not, we need to add, as radically different from Pound's Image or Ideographic radical as Olson thought. It is a spatial configuration, a "mappemund," he calls it, both a formula and formulation of the transactional. It communicates, then, not by bearing a message from sender to receiver or past to present, but as a provocation to the reader-receiver: that is, it provokes an interpretative performance, like that which Lyotard names "agonistics." A poem composes a "field" but an "open field," and may function like a musical text to direct but not quite determine a performance. Thus, every poem is a kind of communicative unit Olson calls a "letter," which like Derrida's postcard bears its message on two disjunct sides, in a double figurality of image and script, each in turn doubled within itself. Olson's glyph-poem organizes space and illustrates, yet does not depict or represent. It cannot be reduced to theme, for its play of marks disrupts rather than orders a grammar. It is a language game indicating that the place of "constitutive inequality" is language itself. Thus his statement that the noun as "graphic Ist" precedes narrative. It motivates narrative, the story we tell of it, which is also the story of its change of value.

The poem as communication unit is, therefore, not a message but a prop and prompt, a performative. It is impromptu. These patterns can be called interpretations if we suspend the notion of interpretation as decodification. For while Olson sought to break the Mayan code, what he really wanted was to find the secret of codification itself. And he seemed to know that it depended on decodification, a critical breaking that would throw the question forward rather than leave one gazing nostalgically upon some long buried and concealed sign of a lost and dead truth. Take the following passage, a "letter" or fragment of correspondence with Robert Creeley which appears in a form no different from Olson's usual line. It is not a letter prompting a response, nor does it necessarily bear a message upon which one can mount a theory. It is a record of a break in thinking, and thus of that very disjunction it names as language:

CONJUNCTION & DISPLACEMENT, the sense of C & D,
D & C, etc. etc. Is verse.
        Is quite another thing than time,
               Is buildings, Is
des ign.
      Is—for our trade—
          THE DISJUNCT, language
in order to occupy space, *be* object (it being so hugely as intervals
TIME) has to be thrown around, re-assembled, in order that it speak,
the man whose interstices it is the re-make of
        ((Is the other side: of Kukulkan
               perhaps?:
      VIOLENCE
                  (*Correspondence*, V, 66–67)

Kukulkan is the name of a Mayan god who engendered maize, but who, like the Egyptian Thoth, is most celebrated for inventing language. He was a "WRITER" and thus the deity of "language and astronomy" or the culture's measuring systems. Whether or not one sees in the "The K," a poem Olson wrote in the name of Kukulkan, the very mark or figure of chiasmus, a differential Mayan notion of "crossing" as violent disjunction, that is what "K's" invention signifies and why he and his culture stand for Olson, in opposition to humanism. The role of this figure is not to compose a center, but to be the one who legislates at some crossing point where invention is "made available to *others*," a point at which there is both conjunction and displacement, as between Riemann's multiplicities or discontinuous surfaces.

"The Kingfishers," another poem inscribing the "K" in its title, is one of Olson's earlier experiments in articulating this notion of deflected crossing, a displacement, as it were, of the Oedipal crossing out of which was composed the dream of western history as family romance. Despite his debt to Pound, and the fact that his own notion of glyph owes considerably to Pound's sense of the Image as "interpretive metaphor," Olson thought Poundian theory and practice to be the modernist culmination of western humanism. Modernism was a humanism, he seemed to conclude with Feidelson, though he viewed its significance differently. Pound's Orientalism seemed designed to close the historical circle by reinstating in western language what it had momentarily forgotten, its scriptive force, but it excluded what stood outside the circle of historicism or, quite simply, outside the circle itself. Thus Olson's desire to "go back" in order to "come forward" evidences once more a postmodern and avant-garde attack upon Man or the subject. We will have to see, on the one hand, whether Olson's is not a move necessary to his redefining the sense of the modern itself, and, on the other, whether Pound does not manifest in theory and practice a certain postmodernism to which Olson is necessarily blind.

Are modernism and postmodernism separate and distinct, or merely useful distinctions? Can they be defined in terms of humanism and the humanitarian or post-humanistic? Lyotard, we might recall, named postmodern that activity which was necessary for the "advent" of the modern: "Postmodernism . . . is not modernism at its end but in its nascent state, and this state is constant"; "The postmodern would be that which, in the modern, put forward the unpresentable in presentation itself, that which denies itself the solace of good forms, the consensus of taste which would make it possible to share collectively the nostalgia for the attainable." The postmodern signifies desire and is manifest in what Lyotard calls the figurality of art, or that which cannot be reduced to conceptuality and therefore to discursive practices. Strangely enough, while he finds postmodernism most forcefully manifest in art and its "critical function," Lyotard says that this critical function characterizes the work of philosophy: "A postmodern artist or writer is in the position of a philosopher: the text he writes, the work he produces are not in principle governed by preestablished rules, and they cannot be judged according to a determining judgement, by applying familiar categories to the text or to the work. The artist and the writer, then, are working without rules in order to formulate the rules of *what will have been done*" (*Postmodern Condition*, 79, 81). Rather than anarchical, he says, the postmodern discordance is a language game which produces the agenda of the new. But because it tends to disturb old categories of understanding (representations) by marking off their purely arbitrary operations, it appears nihilistic and adversarial, and certainly dehumanizing, if not altogether chaotic.

Lyotard cites Joyce as an example of a modernist experiment which "alludes to something which does not allow itself to be made present," thus allowing the "unpresentable to become perceptible" in writing itself. Style asserts its own operations, in excess of any signification, meaning, or theme it might eventually be reduced to. Figure is that which resists our reading the work in terms of old expectancies, as if it were governed by the old rules and categories. But in its reading and exposure of the old conventions, it is fashioning at the same time the possibilities for new representations; not, however, representations or, as Lyotard calls them, "phantasms" of our desire, but displacements of our desire, figures which resist cathexis or our submission to the illusion that they are realities. Art produces figurations that free us and the artist from the illusion that they are representations, as dreams, of our subjective identities, hence realities. They dispossess us of the illusion of humanist depth, and indicate what is beyond either presentation or representation. Hence, Lyotard says, "modernism is an aesthetics of the sublime," a limit marked by the postmodern. Can this be read in a poem like Olson's "The Kingfishers"? A piece of moderate length, it opens with what is evidently a translation of fragment 23 of Heraclitus, as if filtered through Nietzsche: "What does not change / is the will to change." (Note that the slash does not designate a line end but is a part of the line.) The sense of change changes, Olson says, even though the old word remains. How are we to read Heraclitus today, in an age of information theory, without changing him, translating him? that is, submitting to the imperatives of his utterance? Is it possible, as Heidegger thought, to "destructure" ontotheological metaphysics so as to grasp once again the thinking of the pre-Socratics, or is our reading a transcribing, as if through a cybernetic machine, of all the basic words of and for Being? "The Kingfishers" seems to suggest that we do both at the same time, that a poem is always a kind of "double function" described in Olson's letter quoted above. At the poem's conclusion, the poet announces his own effort as archeological rather than philological, an effort to peel away the layers of conceptual thought in order to arrive at something firm ("I hunt among stones") that is not Eliot's church or ontotheological institution, not *logos*, but nevertheless is language, glyph. Yet, archeological reappropriation, which restores the sign as fragment, does not recover a primal sense or scene.

Indeed, the third and concluding section of the poem is an elaborate set of allusions to Eliot's and Pound's logocentric modernism, emphasizing the way Eliot's cooptation of fragments from both pre-history and history, or myth and literature, so as to verify some informing archetype, produces the same paralysis with which he indicts the modern in, say, "The Love Song of J. Alfred Prufrock." When Eliot conjoins the Fisher King and Shakespeare, as in *The Waste Land*, he arraigns them both within a "white mythology" (Derrida). Rimbaud, in contrast, by abandoning poetry for action (performance) signifies the resistance in his own writing to the old economic rules. Rimbaud's poetry and his *agon* are not, like Eliot's, nostalgic. But the major allusion, actually a near quotation, in the last stanza is to/from Pound's first Pisan Canto, number LXXIV:

I pose you your question
shall you uncover honey/where maggots are?

(Writings, 173)

The reference is to Pound's figure of the rotting bodies of "Ben and la Clara" suspended "by the heels at Milano," out of which Pound had drawn some minimal hope that history would survive its heroes because their action, in bringing it to crisis, had in some way engendered a productive activity even if it could not determine efficient ends. Pound had set his own hope for process against Eliot's paralyzing nostalgia: "say this to Possum: a bang, not a whimper—." But Olson's question reads Pound's effort to survive his prison-house of western history as a reaffirmation of the old humanism, a faith in a process that works through man the adventurer, recalling Carlyle's and Emerson's heroes. "The Kingfishers" as a whole parodies the Poundian attempt to contain all of western history in the memory bank of one individual hero, or one canon of texts, one ideology, reassembled in a poem that is both recollection and anthology, process and icon.

But the concluding lines of the poem, like the opening one, inscribe something else. While Pound's historicism is rejected, his own permanent and indelible contribution to poetry is acknowledged in the silent mark or slash, like the one Pound had inserted in Canto LXXIV: "That maggots shd/eat the dead bullock." Olsen literally brackets his own poem with a graphism that Pound had restored to the phonetic tradition of western verse in the form of Imagist and Ideogrammatic writing. It is as if Pound were acknowledging that heterogeneity that the western tradition tried to exclude in its privileging of phonetic writing, even if for Pound this meant recovering a natural language (nature being a system of differential forces). Pound's mark is reinscribed in the first line to separate Heraclitus from the Socratics, and in the last line to bracket a western literary tradition which culminates in "high modernism." It is precisely upon these marks of rupture and transition that Olson locates the turn of his own new poetics, that advent of postmodernism which will trope the tradition. Reinscription, by quotation, allusion, citation—thus Olson repeats the modernist strategy of reappropriation, by revealing the performative power of such language games. As Emerson suggested, quotation and allusion become original and originary acts.

"The Kingfishers" opens in what Harold Bloom would call a Scene of Instruction, evoking a conversation at Black Mountain. It is not, however, the historical or autobiographical reference which is important, but the marking of a performative activity of social exchange, set against Pound's poetic scene of isolation. Moreover, the poet's memory is not narratized, or grammatical, but, both relaxed and animated by alcohol, he is able to make sense of the previous night's drunken conversations by a different and yet unformulated set of rules, a new kind of rhyming. Olson might have thought of it as paratactic rather than hypotactic, metonymic rather than metaphoric. But it is best understood as a dialogic discordance, an undoing of the notion of a continuous or seamless history of meanings. Rambling association rhymes, and underscores the accidence of rhyme, so that the rhyme, which finds similarities in differences is revealed to be the illusory ground of western (humanist) value. Undoubtedly, there had been talk of ancient cultures, and probably of what modern anthropology had done in making them understandable. The poet recalls some talk of a culture where "kingfishers" were at once real and sacred birds, and their feathers valued as a medium of exchange, as against those mythic cultures uncovered or interpreted by Frazer as pre-historical analogs of modern Judeo-Christian cultures. Eliot's appropriation of this model, through Frazer, is just one more example of the western totalitarianism which reduces everything to a representation of its own cyclic myths. Olson's poem wants to break this hermeneutic circle.

The poet's memory is not recollection in tranquility. He recalls fragments as "factors" (the term comes from cybernetics, and may suggest, like Pound's "luminous detail," active fact or "interpretative" signs) whose common denomination is that they are signs or marks the meaning of which is neither self-evident nor stable, though they are necessary for meaning to occur. Where they are inscribed, or reinscribed, they function to produce a significance that is not imminent to them or legislated by any context they may have formerly inhabited. For ex-

ample, he recalls in association with the "feathers" of the
kingfishers, the "E on the stone" at Delphi, and a speech made
by Mao (in French) at a communist rally in 1948, each in its way
signifying a scene of transition and translation, exchange. Mao
is like the oracle of a new culture, though he speaks here the
language of the West. The "E" at Delphi was the legendary
mark of the place of prophecy, whose meaning for modern culture has been translated according to the authority western culture allotted to Petrarch's writing (that is, the philological or
learned tradition), though modern scholars had come to chal-
lenge the Petrarchan interpretation. The point is that all of
these signs are factors which do not contain a stable meaning
but function tropically to provoke readings, or when reinscribed in later contexts, function performatively. They are
tropes of change, and wherever reinscribed they in turn produce change and exchange. They are interpretations that return like feedback in a cybernetic machine, as part of its
necessary noise or entropy, to make possible new information,
though information now deprived of the cognitive authority of
logocentrism. (This reading is verified in section 4 of Part 1,
which deals explicitly with information theory, and makes direct allusion not only to Norbert Wiener's cybernetics but also
indirectly recalls Riemannian mathematics.)

Just as the "E" at Delphi is a sign which cannot be understood
in terms of Petrarch's learned interpretation of it as the Om-
phalos, since that reading only transforms it into an archetypal
model for western thought, its assumption of a "world navel" or
central word in which all thought is grounded, Frazer's and
Eliot's reading of the Fisher King silently tries to confirm what
they already know. Even the scientific description of the bird
(Olson takes it from the *Encyclopaedia Brittanica*) can do no
more than confirm a certain taxonomical explanation and thus
repeat the humanist tradition of ruling by understanding, that
is, logocentrism. And this is what the poem is about—a re-marking of the limits of all systematics, of hermeneutic recuperation,
even as it indicates that nothing lives outside a system and that
no system is exclusive. The law of tropology (of entropy), however, can only be formulated within an economics of limit, a sta-
tistics of calculated loss. What Olson wants to track, to map, is

the apparently violent moment of displacement necessary to move from one system to another, as in Riemann's "multiplicities," or from one mode of thought to another:

When the attentions change/the jungle
leaps in
          even the stones are split
                    they rive
Or,
enter
that other conqueror we more naturally recognize
he so resembles ourselves
But the E
cut so rudely on that oldest stone
sounded otherwise,
was differently heard

It is the use and abuse (the usury) of "factors" that Olson wants to highlight, especially the deadly habit of reducing everything to a singular interpretation, which Olson associates with the "conqueror" or the humanist.

In section 3 of Part 1, Olson inserts a series of quotations from Prescott's *History of the Conquest of Mexico*.[12] They are putative details or objective observations describing a nativist ceremony that the historian had disinterestedly recorded as evidence of a superstitious and hence inferior culture, but that, in Olson's arrangement, turn out to be the signs of a sophisticated kind of grounding, since all grounding must factor death as a non-representational sign into the system. Quoting Prescott, Olson extracts the details from the context of a narratized history and reinscribes them as factors or as that which resists the narrative modality of the historian. At the beginning of Part 11, he returns to Prescott's texts in order to emphasize the difference between poetic and narrative discourse, between "documentary" and totalitarian interpretation. Prescott's reading of history, he suggests, has, in its way, repeated the story of conquest that it tells, by featuring the conquistador Cortez as an instrument of western Enlightenment: the same Cortez who, as Williams had argued in *In the American Grain*, destroyed by expropriation and by imposing alien religious practices on a culture whose forms were otherwise grounded. In contrast, Olson recalls another conquistador, Cabeza de Vaca, who came to conquer, but remained to be assimilated like a factor recycled or fed back into a living history.[13] De Vaca plays for Olson the same role as does Pere Sebastian Rasles for Williams: he becomes a metonymic figure for rewriting America's history. That is, history cannot simply be rewritten from an opposite point of view until one has exposed the totalitarian mechanisms of historicism, thus writing against the grain, diverting the old narrative and its conventions. Cabeza's inscriptions in the American ground make it necessary to write a new history of its history, which is as different from Europe's as Heisenberg's physics is from Newton's. In sum, Olson's quotations function to deconstruct Prescott's historicism.

Olson's poem, then, does more than thematically refute "high modernism" and humanism. His poem critically intervenes by bracketing and highlighting the operations of the modernist text, by presenting its modes of presentation as something not modern at all, unless the whole history of the West is modern. In Olson's view this presentation has the effect of opening the text, so that the question becomes, how does one keep it open: how to resist the same blind collapse back into formalism that modernism seemed to make just as it announced its break with the past? For despite Olson's argument with Pound, it is possible to read in the older poet's attempts to write it new those same postmodern gestures Olson found it necessary to invent in order to pass beyond modernism. We could point to Pound's early criticism, or more specifically to his lifelong revisions of Eliot's notion of tradition. For, Pound's critical practice, like Olson's, reduplicates the poetic performance in the very sense that it inscribes what in early essays he called "luminous detail" and "interpretative metaphor," or a kind of figural economy of writing that serves to dismantle the very tradition it claims to reappropriate. But it is in his advance beyond Imagist practice, in the strategy or performative force of quotation, that is, within his own manner of archeo-semiological assembly, that we can witness the critical or interpretative thrust of Pound's invention, that form of phono-logo-poeia, to combine two of his terms, which serves not to recover some lost word, but to release the potential of the fragment.

We might call upon Canto I as an example, which, as is well known, rewrites or translates a section of the *Odyssey* (from Book II) in an "Amurikun" idiom filtered through Anglo-Saxon conventions. More importantly, the Canto is a translation of a Latin translation, published in Renaissance Paris (1538), and includes in itself a citation of its own itinerary—the itinerary of a translation, a graphic history of its own voyage, a "periplum," as Pound would call it, of literary metamorphosis that cannot be thought on the order of eternal repetition or genealogical history. Though Pound often argued that all great poetry was contemporaneous, this did not mean universal in the idealist sense, but that every great and enduring work would reveal at once its way of being different, of opening up the possibilities of the new. Thus, a beginning in medias res, by translating a text which itself thematizes transformation, indicates that all poems (as voyages, games, re-turns) have always already begun. Translation does not recover meaning but transports it, meta-morphosizes it in the sense of altering its structure, and trans-poses it in the sense of producing a new place or *topos* for the trope.

The Odyssean theme of return, to bury the forgotten Elpenor after a visit to the underworld, is, of course, a kind of literary paradigm of literature, as Pound underscores through-out the unfolding *Cantos*, and not simply an epic convention re-peated in the *Aeneid* or *Divine Comedy*, among others. That is, the theme is not simply an archetype, governing repetition of the same, but a model of repetition with a difference, of begin-ning again. Every return refactors or feeds back into the form certain elements that in turn are projected into a different form, necessitating another journey (not necessarily quest ro-mances), just as Vergil's and Dante's versions mark transitional passages between cultures and in a sense are revisions rather than replicas of the genre. To cite these works is to cite not only the theme of going back to come forward, but to emphasize the supplementary effects of this repetition. Each retelling ad-vances the voyage, or adds by a kind of accidence, that which was not inscribed in the destiny of the original. Original force is already belated, and belongs to feedback. Pound does not stress an entropic history of language and culture, like Eliot's decline of the West through falling towers, from the purity of classical Greek through Latin to the modern. (Though Pound does find an exhaustion or softening in Latinity.) On the contrary, he celebrates those points where the vulgate or idiomatic feeds back into the learned and formal to reinvigorate a stagnating system, the ontotheological orthodoxy. Homer and Ovid and Dante and Chaucer and Whitman are respectively modern writers who supervise the idiomatic reinsemination of literature. They are metonyms of interpretive translation itself, since what they name is the discordance of invention or the double writing evident in every new or inventive text. A new genre is nothing more than an anthology of earlier genres, a heterogeneous collection of old rules or factors.

Therefore, when Pound transcribes the story of Elpenor, he marks the originary moment of art as language or figure, as that which bears old meanings and forms on its back and points forward to new uses, transcribing paleonymic words into new functions. The "And" that inaugurates the poem translates the place of origin as a margin, as "Conjunction and Displacement," to recall Olson. In Canto II, the poem leaps forward from Homer and the Homeric Hymns (not authored by Homer but which Pound discovered to be arbitrarily appended to the Latin text he had bought in Paris, and out of which he took the Elpenor section) to Browning's poetic retelling of the history of a minor Italian poet-figure, a name who also appears in Dante's underworld as someone the poet consulted in his own version of the "eternal return." The reference to Sordello carries back to Homer and Helen, who preceded and motivated Odysseus' voyage, and comes forward through Aeschylus' inscription of Helen's name in a pun for "destruction." Quoting Aeschylus, Pound, in his turn, inscribes the historical and Anglicized name of Eleanor of Aquitaine into the game, thus rhyming myth and history in a curious plot or transaction that disturbs our distinction between the two. Thus "*helandros, helenaus*, and *heleptolis*" (to transcribe the Greek of Aeschylus into phonemic equivalences) bears the very force of displacement it ascribes to the proper name. If the historical Eleanor was in fact a "destroyer" of cities, men, and ships, as Aeschylus played upon the character inscribed in Helen's name, she was also the seminal force behind a history that included a promotion of the arts (she was both a matron and patron of Provencal poetry), and a founding of noble lineage (she was a mother of a line of English kings). She completes not only the odyssey of history from Greece to Rome to France to England, but also that from classical to medieval to Renaissance, from epic to tragic to comic, to that modern verge to be fulfilled in Shakespeare's invention of the history play out of the generic fragments that were to be the Renaissance's inheritance. Pound's Eleanor, therefore, functions as a disseminating figure, as the heterogeneous force of styles. She is the metonym of genesis, of figuration, of the performative force of quotation—of appropriation itself. Unlike the hermaphroditic Tiresias of Eliot she is not a passive voyeur but an active, destructive-creative force. Like Helen in H.D.'s Helen, "she is the writing." We should also recall here that Helen is inscribed in Canto I not only as the motivating force of the *Odyssey*, but also as the marginal figure of the Latin text that compels Pound's own translation. For Divus's learned displacement of the Greek has been produced in Paris, as part of the Gutenberg galaxy, and was itself a kind of anthology. Canto I cites the place of production as a kind of transposition, and at the same time notes that the Renaissance text had as appendix certain so-called hymns in praise of Helen's beauty, that sensuous figurality that compels all writing. And so *The Cantos* is launched on what Stevens called a "sea of ex," or a metaphorics of displacement.

In Canto III, Pound makes a transition that leads to reflections on "Myo Cid," that is, to the question of the status of a belated epic like *El Cid*, pointing out not only the problematic relation between epic and history, literature and reality, as Bakhtin would later note, but making it evident that no genre remains in itself stable and canonical. Just as "the" Cid becomes "My" Cid, the Sordello of Canto II had become "my Sordello," a factor reappropriated from both history and literature, via the underground allegory of Dante and the modern psychologism of Browning, to become once more the object of interpretation and the name of interpretative force. Canto VII repeats this history of displacements, by and of the letter, in terms of the "Si pulvis nullus / Erit, nullum tamen excute" of Ovid (whose metamorphic deconstruction of the epic and dramatic had dominated the larger part of Canto II), and the "e li mestiers ecoutes" of Bertrand de Born. Both Ovidian and Provencal writing are celebrated for their uncovering, not of some past and forgotten meaning, but of the power of writing to move, transform, or bring to light: for their displacement of tradition, their tradition of displacement. Thus every new writer invents by unlayering, or touching again the living, fertile body—of figurality itself. Canto VII, therefore, provides an index of metonyms for this disfiguration and displacement of styles. Homer, Ovid, Bertrand, Dante, Flaubert, and Henry James are arraigned not as a history of texts but as an intertextual adventure, each turning or troping the other, like Dante confronting Sordello, or Pound confronting the "voice" of James weaving an "endless sentence." *The Cantos* is a condensed anthology, a *periplus* of misprison, an allegory of reading.

Are we ready now to say just where Pound has marked, or re-marked, the false genetic moment of his song, the transitional or transactional, that is, the translative moment he had as early as *The Spirit of Romance* named "interpretative translation"? It would not be a moment at all—or, to put it otherwise, it would be originary and not original, like Emerson's "quotation." It is there, already inscribed, in the metonyms which allow him to move easily from myth to history, or from Dante's Sordello to "my Sordello"; from the inhumed Elpenor of Homer to the Helen whose name and mythic role, whose legend, had endangered the epic recounting of a history and adventure in which Elpenor is a mere turning point, or from mythic Helen to the historical Eleanor. That is, everything turns upon the "constitutive equivocality" of the phoneme or morpheme "el," which functions like Olson's "factor" feeding back into Pound's repeated beginnings and leaps, his conjunctions and displacements. Elpenor, Helen, Eleanor, Sordello, Myo (El) Cid, even the possum, Eliot, indirectly invoked in Canto VIII and directly misquoted in Canto LXXIV. The "el" which can variously recall the force of the ancient Hebrew deity, the pluralized god *Elo*-him, or as Canto VII reminds us, the reappearance of the *Ely*sian field on a Parisian bus: a "date for peg" as Pound calls such fragments. Can the *Ele*usinian mysteries be irrelevant to

The Cantos, not as source or reference but only as another name for language? Is the "el" not a morphemic signature of the "constitutive equivocality" of a writing that has always already begun, the postmodern mark of an origin which like Derrida's *différance* can bear no proper name and is older than Being? Or as Wallace Stevens would say: "The the"? Certainly, Pound's translations of these notes from underground are without reference, and they produce an infinite possibility of a text that he would finally call a palimpsest.

But one cannot possibly go on reading these diverging yet crossing lines, except to re-mark them in another language. Pound's poem reminds us again of Derrida's admonition to the translator, that there are always "two languages in language" and that "living on" in language always requires a passage through the unrepresentable place of death. The task of the poet-translator and that of deconstruction predicates such an unmappable itinerary. Why do I hear at this moment the Valéryean exclamation, "tel quel," "just as it is," or just as it was appropriated for the name of the poststructural revolution? And within that echo, another, "Qual Quelle," Derrida's title for his essay on Valéry's "sources" (in *Margins,* pp. 273-306). *Qual Quelle,* is it a reference to or quotation from Hegel, out of Boehme? It is certainly Hegel's translation of Boehme, the Hegelian formulation that negativity does not issue from a falling away from origin but strangely enough constitutes the source. Negativity is consciousness, is origin, a source produced in the moment it is cut off from being and is reappropriated, as it were, on the rebound. Derrida's word for this strange constitutive source, which is not an origin, is *relever,* which indicates constitution by de-constitution, by negation and sublation, restoring by raising up again a source that is originally discontinuous, heterogeneous, and marked by alterity: a source (*Quelle*) already marked by torment or pain (*Qual*), originarily negated like a deity who is the Devil or a poem speaking from Hell. It is no wonder that Pound, who began his poem by quoting Homer, concludes it by nominating its author as a "Disney against the metaphysicals," a parodist of the imagination.

Notes

Chapter One

1. Translated as "The Ends of Man," in *Margins of Philosophy*, translated with additional notes by Alan Bass (Chicago: University of Chicago Press, 1982), pp. 109–36. Hereafter noted in the text as *Margins*.
2. *The Fate of Reading and Other Essays* (Chicago: Univ. of Chicago Press, 1975), p. 107.
3. *The Question of Being*, translated with introduction by William Kluback and Jean T. Wilde (New Haven, CT: College and University Press, 1958), p. 105. Hereafter noted in text as QB.
4. *Being and Time*, translated by John Macquarrie and Edward Robinson (New York: Harper and Row, 1962). Hereafter noted in text as BT.
5. See "Ousia et Gramme," in *Margins*, p. 63.
6. *Blindness and Insight* (New York: Oxford University Press, 1971), pp. 29-32, 76, 100.
7. In *Poetry, Language, Thought*, translated with introduction by Albert Hofstadter (New York: Harper and Row, 1971), pp. 17–87. Hereafter noted in text as PLT.
8. *What Is Called Thinking*, translated by Fred D. Wieck and J. Glenn Gray (New York: Harper Torchbooks, 1968). Cited in text as WICT.
9. *On the Way to Language*, translated by Peter D. Hertz (New York: Harper and Row, 1971). Cited in text as OWTL.
10. *Existence and Being*, translated with introduction and analysis by Werner Brock (Chicago: Regnery, 1949). Cited in text as EB.
11. In *Disseminations*, translated with introduction and additional notes by Barbara Johnson (Chicago: University of Chicago Press, 1981), pp. 173–285.

Chapter Two

1. All references to Freud come from *The Standard Edition of the Complete Psychological Works of Sigmund Freud*, 24 vols., translated and edited by James Strachey et al. (London: Hogarth Press, 1953).
2. Quotations from H.D.'s work, hereafter cited in the text, are from the following texts: *Trilogy* (New York: New Directions, 1973); *Tribute to*

Freud (Boston: Godline, 1974), hereafter *Tribute*; *Helen in Egypt*, introduction by Horace Gregory (New York: New Directions, 1961); and *Hermetic Definition* (New York: New Directions, 1972).

3. *Spurs/Éperons*, translated by Barbara Harlow (Chicago: University of Chicago Press, 1978), pp. 107, 81.

4. Clemence Ramnoux, *Héraclite, ou l'homme entre les choses et les mots* (Paris: Société d'Édition Les Belle Lettres, 1968), pp. 302–4.

5. [Editor's note: This postscript was written at the request of an editor who wished to include this previously published essay in a collection on *American Critics at Work: Examinations of Contemporary Literary Theories*, edited by Victor Kramer (Troy, NY: Whitson Publishing Company, 1984).]

6. In *Deconstruction and Criticism* (New York: Seabury Press, 1979), pp. 75–176. The footnote "Border Lines" runs along the entire lower edge of the lengthy primary text, a text that, one notes, puts in question the very notion of a *primary* text, or indicates that the phrase is already an oxymoron. The two texts, essay and note, repeatedly engage in a commentary not only on other texts but on the question of commentary, and hence across the boundaries which would discreetly maintain a hierarchy of texts and commentaries. This breaching of boundaries and frontiers stages the question of quotation, citation, commentary, translation, and so on, both as a strategy and as a commentary on strategy. Thus it is difficult to determine the status of what appears to be a meta-commentary or an ontological statement such as the one I have just quoted.

7. *Deconstruction and Criticism*, p. 77n. Much of Derrida's writing touches on this "economical" yet pleonastic notion of "translation." See, for example, "The *Retrait* of Metaphor," translated in *Enclitic* 2 (Fall 1978): 5–33.

Chapter Three

1. See Paul de Man, "Sign and Symbol in Hegel's *Aesthetics*," *Critical Inquiry* 8 (Summer, 1982), 761–75.

2. See *Collected Poems of Wallace Stevens* (New York: Knopf, 1954).

3. *The Philosophy of History*, translated by J. Sibree (New York: Dover, 1956), pp. 86-87.

4. *The Complete Works of Ralph Waldo Emerson*, 12 vols., edited by Edward Waldo Emerson (Boston: Harcourt Brace Jovanovich, 1971). "Circles" appears in volume II.

5. *Glas* (Paris: Galilee, 1974), p. 15, left column; and passim (my translation).

6. Walt Whitman, *Leaves of Grass: Comprehensive Reader's Edition*, edited by Harold W. Blodgett and Sculley Bradley (New York: New York University Press, 1965), p. 55.

7. *The Collected Poems of Hart Crane*, edited with introduction by Waldo Frank (New York: Liveright Publishing Corp., 1933), p. 136.

8. *Hegel's Aesthetics: Lectures on Fine Art*, vol. I (London: Oxford University Press, 1975), pp. 303ff.

9. See *The Cantos of Ezra Pound* (New York: New Directions, 1970).

10. Oswald Spengler, *The Decline of the West* . . . , 2 vols., translated by Charles Atkinson (New York: Knopf, 1926-28).

11. "Foreshadowing and Foreshortening: The Prophetic Vision of Origins in Hart Crane's *The Bridge*," *Word & Image* 1 (July–September, 1985): 288–312.

12. The designer of the Brooklyn Bridge, John Roebling, was, as scholars have shown, a follower of Hegel, and he conceived of its structure in dialectical terms. Crane, who happened to occupy Roebling's apartment near the Bridge after the designer's death, thought of Roebling as a genius-visionary who had resolved the phenomenological problem of translating vision into spatial form. See Alan Trachtenberg, *Brooklyn Bridge: Fact and Symbol* (New York: Oxford University Press, 1965; Chicago: University of Chicago Press, 1979).

Chapter Four

1. Quotations from Stein are from the following texts and will be subsequently cited in the text as follows:

HW—*How to Write* (New York: Dover, 1975)

GHA—*The Geographical History of America* (New York: Vintage, 1973)

MA—*The Making of Americans* (New York: Something Else Press, 1966)

LA—*Lectures in America* (Boston: Beacon Press, 1985)

SW—*Selected Writings of Gertrude Stein*, edited by Carl Van Vechten, with an essay by F.F. Dupee (New York: Vintage, 1972)

2. Friedrich Nietzsche, *The Will to Power*, translated by Walter Kaufmann and R.J. Hollingdale (New York: Vintage, 1967), no. 487, p. 269.

3. Wyndham Lewis, *Time and Western Man* (Boston: Beacon Press, 1957), p. 86; first published in 1927. Also see, Jacques Maritain, *Bergsonian Philosophy and Thomism*, translated by Maybelle Anderson and J. Gordon Anderson (New York: Greenwood Press, 1968); published in 1914 as *La philosophie Bergsonienne*, and revised and reissued several times subsequently. T.E. Hulme's embrace of and resistance to Bergson, somewhat like Eliot's, in essays such as "Romanticism and Classicism," "Bergson's Theory of Art," and "Intensive Manifolds," are collected in *Speculations*, edited by Herbert Read (New York: Harcourt Brace, 1924), would seem to owe much to Maritain's analysis of Bergson's romanticism.

4. See Kathryne V. Lindberg, *Reading Pound Reading: Modernism After Nietzsche* (New York: Oxford University Press, 1987), for a careful and

discriminating analysis of the difference between Pound and Eliot, not only in their notions of the force of tradition, but also their differing sense of the fate of the post-Nietzschean writing subject. Also see Maud Ellmann, *The Poetics of Impersonality: T.S. Eliot and Ezra Pound* (Cambridge, MA: Harvard University Press, 1987) for an examination of Eliot's Bergsonism.

5. See Gilles Deleuze, *Bergsonism*, translated by Hugh Tomlinson and Barbara Habberjam (New York: Zone, 1988); first published in 1966 as *Le Bergsonisme*, and later revised and expanded.

6. Quotations from Bergson are from the following books and will be subsequently cited in the text as follows:

CM—*A Study in Metaphysics: The Creative Mind* (Totowa, NJ: Littlefield, Adams, 1965)

MM—*Matter and Memory*, translated by N.M. Paul and W.W. Palmer (New York: Zone, 1988)

CE—*Creative Evolution*, translated by Arthur Mitchell (New York: Henry Holt, 1911)

In *Creative Evolution*, where Bergson discusses the materialization of mind as a kind of "congealing" of spirit or elan, he indicates that poetic creation or an imaginative "act of mind" manifests itself as a type of pause in which process breaks up into dissociated forms: "letters which are added to all the letters there are already in the world" (CE, 253). In this sense, words would seem to be the product of an evolution, and not fixities retentive of past meanings or memories. Manifest language, he says in *Matter and Memory*, "whether elaborated or crude, leaves many more things to be understood than it is able to express. Essentially discontinuous, since it proceeds by juxtaposing words, speech can only indicate by a few guideposts placed here and there the chief guideposts in the movement of thought" (MM, 125). Discursive intellect works in discontinuous phases while the creative operates by a process of combining and relating images, past and present (though no images are strictly past), in the motor process that will eventually appear in the "congealed" form of language when the process makes its "pause": "Order is . . . a certain agreement between subject and object. It is mind finding itself again in things" (CE, 235). The creative act is a process of "disorder," as it were; and here Bergson would seem to be echoing the metaphors of the stochastic theory of thermodynamics. Order, it would seem, is the process of coming to a kind of self-reflective consciousness, a slowing down of the act of the mind into selected and juxtaposed images, words, letters. But he resists the model of language for the creative process, and finds it rather in the "discursive intellect."

7. See Derrida, "Fors: The English Words of Nicholas Abraham and Maria Torok," translated by Barbara Johnson, a foreword to Abraham and Torok, *The Wolf Man's Magic Words: A Cryptonomy*, translated by

Nicholas Rand (Minneapolis: University of Minnesota Press, 1986), pp. xi–xviii.

8. See Deleuze, *Cinema 1, The Movement Image*, translated by Hugh Tomlinson and Barbara Habbarjam (Minneapolis: University of Minnesota Press, 1986). Here, as in his *Bergsonism*, Deleuze gives us a contemporary, poststructural Bergson, deflecting in a certain way the metaphysics that Heidegger and Derrida find ineradicable from the Bergsonian process, from his notion of time and the multiple unity of interiority.

9. *Bergsonism*, pp. 39–40. Deleuze does not amplify on Bergson's appropriation of the Riemannian mathematical model, beyond pointing out the philosopher's own early training in science, and his effort to move philosophy as a human science beyond the limitations he found in the scientific description of the world. We have noted Bergson's response to Einstein, and his argument that Einsteinian time, the fourth dimension, remained spatial and quantitative. Einstein, of course, was highly indebted to Riemann's formulations of planal transformations, as was Buckminster Fuller later, especially in his formulations of the integrity and stability of geodesic structures. But what is at issue here is far from a question of influence or debt in the limited sense of these notions, and different even from the question of what is involved when one domain of conceptualization or one discipline (say, philosophy) borrows its metaphors from another (say, physics or mathematics), where the latter appears more authoritative, legitimate, and true to the nature of things than the former.

10. For Williams's reading of Poe, see *In the American Grain*, introduction by Horace Gregory (New York: New Directions, 1956), pp. 216–33.

Chapter Five

1. In his lectures on Nietzsche's aesthetics Heidegger explores the manner in which Nietzsche transvalues such notions as the "classical," along with other "basic" concepts. "*Basic words are historical*," he argues, and are modified from discipline to discipline, and according to the force of each inquiry. Therefore, common concepts do not remain the same or stable from time to time, or culture to culture. See *The Will to Power as Art*, vol. I of *Nietzsche*, translated by David Farrell Krell (New York: Harper and Row, 1979), p. 144. Certainly, modernism is one of those basic words which today means differently in different areas of inquiry, say, in politics, aesthetics, historicism. Derrida would argue that this change of sense is not simply the choice of a writer, subject, or user of the term, but that reinscription and recontextualization belong to language, and are perhaps its law, though a law that it cannot for-

mulate. In one sense, modernism, if not postmodernism, is a name, though not a proper name, for such changes. It may be easier to speak of modern and postmodern as a "condition," as Jean-Francois Lyotard does in *The Postmodern Condition: A Report on Knowledge*, translated by Geoff Bennington and Brian Massumi (Minneapolis: University of Minnesota Press, 1984), a work that develops a distinction Lyotard drew earlier in *Discours, Figure* (Paris: Klincksieck, 1971), and that I will discuss momentarily.

2. For historians, and even literary critics in general, modernism may mean the whole field of cultural formations named the "Renaissance and after," just as Cartesianism opens modern thought and philosophy. Thus modernism has always in one way or another been identified with self-consciousness, dualism, and even technology. And I would further note, for example, the difference today when modernism is discussed in the context of aesthetics or even literary history, especially in terms of the philosophical problematics articulated by Paul de Man, and when it is discussed in the context of politico-critical discourse, as in the explorations of a "political unconscious" carried out by Fredric Jameson in his studies of writers and thinkers like Wyndham Lewis, or in his explorations of the complicity between modern (and even postmodern) art and architecture and post-industrial capitalism.

3. See Ralph Waldo Emerson, *Journals and Miscellaneous Notebooks*, edited by William H. Gilman et al. (Cambridge, MA: Belknap Press of Harvard University Press, 1960), VIII, 303.

4. See *The Will to Power as Art*, pp. 171–220, for Heidegger's discussion of Kant's Platonism and Nietzsche's overturning of that Platonism, his uncovering of what Heidegger calls the "Raging Discordance between Art and Truth." Although Heidegger persists in finding such "inversions" of metaphysics a return to metaphysics on Nietzsche's part, his own emphasis on "discord" stresses the historical "function" of art in keeping structures "open" as well as its more reified and idealized, if not Platonized, function in the "unconcealment" of Being. Deconstruction radicalizes the "discord" while pointing up Heidegger's problem in separating from *aletheia*.

5. *Logique du sens* (Paris: Minuit, 1969), especially the section of an appendix entitled "Platon et le simulacre," 292–307.

6. Poststructuralist theory in general has been identified with nihilism because of its general attack on all systematics or methodologies, not simply for its rejection of a metaphysics of presence. Of course the argument that all post-philosophical sciences remained metaphysical, and thus were self-deceived in their claims to pass beyond metaphysics, is most obviously identified with deconstruction, the most unregenerately nihilistic of modern philosophies in the view of even those who profess a pragmaticist attitude toward the philosophy of presence. Derrida has persistently refuted these charges of ni-

hilism, and argued instead that, in the wake of Nietzsche's nihilism, it-self a transvaluation of the negative that haunts metaphysics from Plato to Hegel, deconstruction is affirmative. But to its critics, any affirmation of dissemination, whether of heterogeneity, or what Bakhtin called "heterology," flirts with chaos. Heidegger's recognition of the "discord" between beauty and truth marked what systematic phi-losophy had to repress. But deconstruction, far from revelling (as Bakhtin says of the comic or carnivalistic) in increasing rulelessness, or privileging chaos over cosmos, reveals the impossibility of thinking outside the law (outside metaphysics) or structure. Instead, in accord with such marginal thought as Godel's in mathematics or Heisenberg's in physics, it attempts to find some new rule of the rule, or, as Derrida says, some "theory of errata" that will inscribe the limit without over-coming it and returning to totalization and the totalitarian. One re-calls that in the wake of cybernetics and the early developments of information theory certain areas of the critical arts tried to develop a theory of "pataphysics" (borrowing Alfred Jarry's term) which could write a theory of "chaosmos" (Joyce's). But there persists the kind of thinking that argues either/or, *either* cosmos or chaos. Thus, when de-construction begins to question the dream of the social sciences to pass beyond metaphysics, the questioning is perceived as a pure scepti-cism and a dangerously non-serious (or anti-philosophical) mode of thought. Heidegger points out that any humanism must remain meta-physical, or that Nietzsche's inversion of Platonism produces the last metaphysician, Nietzsche himself. Still, Heidegger's own afffirmation of Being seems to redeem him for philosophy, that is, for that which must think "beyond" itself. Derrida outlines a different (to some, per-verse) version of Platonism and the question of Being in *The Post Card: From Socrates to Freud and Beyond*, translated with an introduction by Alan Bass (Chicago: University of Chicago Press, 1987).

7. In a provocative essay first published in the *Atlantic* (1967), John Barth called the parodic metafiction of Borges, "The Literature of Ex-haustion," a term that critics chose to exploit for its purely negative connotations. A decade later, he sought to correct this reading in an-other *Atlantic* piece, "The Literature of Replenishment." These essays are now collected in *The Friday Book* (New York: Putnam, 1984), a text in which Barth stages a scene of reading that virtually dissolves the margins between literature and criticism, or indicates the postmodern imbrication of the one with the other. But for Barth, the postmodern was always already inscribed in the beginning of "story," which always had to include a "story of story." Thus, the literature of "exhaustion" sought to exploit the performative resources of "telling."

8. Harold Rosenberg, *The Tradition of the New* (New York: Horizon Press, 1959).

9. Feidelson, *Symbolism and American Literature* (Chicago: University of Chicago Press, 1954). See also the influential essay or series of essays

by Joseph Frank, entitled "Spatial Form in Modern Literature," which first appeared in the *Sewanee Review* (1945), one of the major journals of the New Criticism, later collected in Frank's *The Widening Gyre* (New Brunswick, NJ: Rutgers University Press, 1963).

10. For a reading of radical self-reflexivity in *Pierre*, see Edgar Dryden, "The Entangled Text: Melville's Pierre and the Problem of Reading," *boundary 2* 7 (1979): 145–73.

11. A short version of the correspondence between Olson and Creeley, called "Mayan Letters," appears in Olson's *Selected Writings* (New York: New Directions, 1966), as does the poem examined at length here, "The Kingfishers." For an extended version of the correspondence, see *Charles Olson & Robert Creeley: The Complete Correspondence*, edited by George Butterick, 8 vols. (Santa Barbara, CA: Black Sparrow Press, 1980).

12. William Hickling Prescott, *History of the Conquest of Mexico; and History of the Conquest of Peru* (New York: Modern Library, 1939).

13. For an account of Cabeza de Vaca's incorporation into the American scene, see Tzvetan Todorov, *The Conquest of America*, translated by Richard Howard (New York: Harper and Row, 1984).

Index